The Power of Tests

LANGUAGE IN SOCIAL LIFE SERIES

Series Editor: Professor Christopher N Candlin

Chair Professor of Applied Linguistics

Department of English

Centre for English Language Education & Communication Research

City University of Hong Kong, Hong Kong

For a complete list of books in this series see pages *v* and *vi*

The Power of Tests

A Critical Perspective on the Uses of Language Tests

Elana Shohamy

An imprint of **Pearson Education**

Harlow, England · London · New York · Reading, Massachusetts · San Francisco · Toronto · Don Mills, Ontario · Sydney
Tokyo · Singapore · Hong Kong · Seoul · Taipei · Cape Town · Madrid · Mexico City · Amsterdam · Munich · Paris · Milan

Pearson Education Limited
Edinburgh Gate
Harlow
Essex CM20 2JE
England

and Associated Companies throughout the world

Visit us on the World Wide Web at:
www.pearsoneduc.com

First published 2001

© Pearson Education Limited 2001

The right of Elana Shohamy to be identified as author of
this work has been asserted by her in accordance with
the Copyright, Designs and Patents Act 1988.

ISBN 0-582-42336-8 CSD
ISBN 0-582-42335-X PPR

British Library Cataloguing-in-Publication Data

A catalogue record for this book is available from the British Library

Library of Congress Cataloging-in-Publication Data

A catalog record for this book is available from the Library of
Congress

Set in 10/12pt Janson by 35
Produced by Pearson Education Asia Pte Ltd.
Printed in Singapore

LANGUAGE IN SOCIAL LIFE SERIES

Series Editor: Professor Christopher N Candlin
Chair Professor of Applied Linguistics
Department of English
Centre for English Language Education & Communication Research
City University of Hong Kong, Hong Kong

For Daphna and Orlee,
    My wonderful daughters,
        My closest friends,
            My most stimulating colleagues

'. . . isn't it possible to have testing of the people, for the people, and by the people?'
(John Oller, Personal communication, 26 May 1998)

Contents

Introduction

Personal biographies are instrumental in one's future. Banks (1998: 6) notes that there is a 'need to better understand and to make explicit the biographical journeys and values of researchers so that we can more closely approach the aim of objectivity in social science research'. It is therefore of no surprise that not doing well on tests motivated me to try to understand the mystery of testing from a different perspective – that of the test taker. My training is in traditional testing. This is where I learned about the psychometric truth of one correct answer. Yet my perspective of testing has always been that of the test taker, attempting to understand why so many of us could not do well on certain types of test, especially those involving multiple-choice items. My early years in language testing focused therefore on research that examined the effect of different contextual variables on scores that test takers obtained on tests. That research showed that variables such as the method of testing did, in fact, affect performance of test takers on tests.

It was a few years later that I learned that none of that really mattered, as the content of the test was not directly related to its use. The 'moment of truth' occurred at a meeting with officials of the Ministry of Education in Israel in 1985, in a discussion surrounding the introduction of a new test of English as a Foreign Language at the end of secondary school. The main principle of this new test was to offer high school students the opportunity to demonstrate their oral proficiency through a number of different elicitation procedures. It was at that meeting that it became clear to me that the psychometric traits of the test – reliability and validity – were irrelevant to the national inspector who was responsible for introducing the test. He was not interested in whether the test gave more accurate results. Rather, his main concern was how the test would affect the teaching of spoken language in the classroom. For him the test had one purpose – a tool through which teachers could be 'made' to teach oral language. His support of the new test was motivated by its potential effects – 'now, teachers will have no choice but to teach students to *speak* English'. That, it turned out, had been his agenda for some time, trying desperately to introduce spoken language into the English classroom but with no success. The test, then, could serve as the tool for making the agenda come true. All the rest was irrelevant. It did not matter that teachers were not trained in teaching spoken language, or that there was no curriculum geared for teaching it. He was convinced that the test and its power would take care of everything.

It was then, and at similar meetings since, that I learned that the quality of a test did not have much to do with its uses, but a lot to do with control – with making teachers and students practise something that those who introduce the tests perceive to be important. The test, through its power, was simply a tool, a means to ensure that words were turned into actions.

It was then that I also learned that policy makers and test developers had different agendas regarding tests; they each viewed tests through very different eyes. Testers believe that the main criterion for good testing is that the tests they construct possess features that provide an indication that they can measure accurately. Policy makers, on the other hand, view tests as a means of promoting educational agendas. The issue, then, is not the tests, but rather their uses.

This realization was a turning point in my testing career as I began to notice how naive and detached testers were from the 'real world' of the use of tests. At that time I could not recall one discussion at the language-testing circles, at conferences, in journals or colloquia, that focused on the motives and uses of tests and on their social and political impacts. Testers, I realized, were not concerned with how tests were being used after they had been constructed; for testers, the use of tests was irrelevant.

Once I began to focus on the use of tests I observed the many ways that tests were used in education and society, not only to force teachers to teach and students to learn but also to impose policies, define knowledge and, worse, to punish, exclude, gate-keep and perpetuate existing powers. Those observations turned into an obsession as I started to pursue the 'why' of testing, putting the 'how' on the back burner. Whenever I was exposed to a new test, I needed to find out the rationale and motivation for introducing it. Why is the test being introduced? What are the motives behind it? What are the agendas? Whose agendas are being followed? What are the real motives for using the test? What is the politics behind it? Who is pushing what and why? Who is interested in the results and why? What is the political constellation that created the need for the test? What are the expected outcomes? I quickly learned that there was an official story and a real story. The official story was that tests were used for educational purposes, to measure knowledge, while the real story in a large number of cases was that the tests were used as a means of achieving certain objectives.

A few years later I had the opportunity to observe another case close-up. The occasion was the introduction of a new national test of reading comprehension. When the results were disseminated they showed that half of all 4th grade students in the country had failed the test. Finding it difficult to accept that such a big proportion of the population could not read, I was not surprised to discover that the results had nothing to do with the test's level of difficulty. It was also clear, as testers know, that 'half' or any other cutting point can be very arbitrary. I again began to ask questions: Why was the test being given at the first place? What was the agenda that drove the introduction of the test? What were the politics of the test? Who was to gain and who was to lose? What was the political motive? What was the relationship among the different bodies that administered it? How would the results be used? How would it affect teaching? What did the test mean for the test takers, their parents, their schools? What were the long- and short-range consequences of the test for the lives of individuals? What did the test do to the knowledge being assessed?

It became clear that testing reading comprehension was only a means, an excuse, for other agendas. The test was used by different bodies as a tool to control, screen, classify, group, punish, threaten, and demonstrate authority. In the summer of 1993 I wrote my first paper on the topic for a conference on Rhetorics (Shohamy, 1994). The paper discussed the rhetorics of the reading comprehension test, pointing to the gap between the declared purpose of the test and its actual use. While the purpose of the test, as expressed in official documents of the Ministry of Education, seemed educational and ethical, the actual uses and consequences were not.

In recent years I have been conducing research in the area of language policy. Professor Bernard Spolsky and I were asked to propose a new language policy for Israel. Given my background and interest in language testing, I again learned about the power of tests as it became clear to me that the 'language testing policy' was the *de facto* 'language policy'. Further, no policy change can take place without a change in testing policy as the testing policy becomes the *de facto* language policy. It was clear that documents and statements about language policy were marginal in comparison to the power of the testing policy. I thus concluded that through the study of testing practices it is possible to learn about the existing educational policies. It was then that I realized what an excellent mirror tests could be for studying the real priorities of those in power and authority, as these are embedded in political, social, educational and economic contexts. It was also then that I decided to study how language tests are used and to focus on the intentions of those in authority in using tests, as well as the effects and consequences of using tests for education and society.

Thus, this book is not about tests but rather about their uses. It presents research, observations and thoughts in an attempt to understand why tests have assumed such powerful roles in modern societies. The book develops a theoretical framework of analysis of the uses and roles of tests in political, social and economic contexts based on empirical studies, real-life cases and voices of test takers. It provides a critique of such uses and offers strategies for controlling and minimizing such uses by developing critical perspectives and proposing democratic models of assessment that consider the responsibilities of testers and the rights of test takers.

Inspirations

This book summarizes ideas, research and thoughts that have occupied me for a long time. Yet ideas do not emerge in a vacuum; rather they are inspired by talks, conversations, discussions, debates, observations and reflections.

Perhaps the most important context in which my thoughts on this topic were formulated was that of the ACROLT (Academic Committee for Research on Language Testing) meetings in Israel. It was in ACROLT that my understanding of the intentions and effects of tests began to emerge. It was through discussions, debates and deliberations that scepticism as to the rationale for introducing tests and their uses surfaced. It was at those meetings, which often included scholars from other countries, that discussions regarding the uses, misuses and abuses of tests began to take shape. It was at those meetings that I started to understand the role of tests within political, social and economic contexts.

It was then that Bernard Spolsky inspired me, and other participants, to pose challenging questions regarding the moral dilemmas that testers face. Of special relevance was Spolsky's book *Measured Words* (1995) pointing to the social and political dimensions of language tests in historical perspectives and the illusion that psychometrics can solve it all.

The never-ending conversations with my close friend and colleague David Nevo have been a major source for understanding the psychology and politics of testing. David's deep insight into the politics and sociology of education, and the central role that tests play in educational policy as bureaucratic tools, provided an understanding of the motives behind the introduction of tests. I am grateful to David for introducing me to the collaborative model presented in the book.

For a number of years I felt that my colleagues in language testing did not appreciate my ideas concerning the uses and consequences of tests. Thus, the invitation by Mary McGroarty to present a plenary talk on Critical Language Testing at the 1997 American Association of Applied Linguistics conference in Orlando, Florida, was interpreted by me as recognition of the importance and relevance of these issues. The favourable reactions to the paper on the part of my colleagues in applied linguistics, as well as many language testers, provided the prime inspiration for writing this book.

A constant source of inspiration are my graduate students and colleagues at Tel Aviv University and in other universities throughout the world (USA, Australia, Canada, Hong Kong, Finland, Denmark, Belgium, Sweden) where I have been invited to lecture and teach courses on issues of the uses of tests. Some of the studies reported in this book were conducted collaboratively with these students and colleagues. I am grateful to them for their ideas, questions, criticism, disagreements and challenges.

While I was in the midst of writing this book I was invited (along with Geoff Brindley, Hussein Farhady, Stan Jones, Tim McNamara, Bonny Norton, Pauline Rea and Peter Skehan) to participate in a summer institute at Carleton University in Ottawa on the topic of 'The social responsibility of the language testers'. The visit to the institute was a very unique experience as it involved faculty and graduate students learning together, trying to understand social and political issues of the use of tests by focusing on the tester, the test taker and other stakeholders. Unlike other academic meetings, this one offered the opportunity to share ideas, ask questions and reflect on moral and ethical dilemmas for six full days. I am grateful to Ian Pringle, Janna Fox and Martha Jenning for organizing such an inspiring meeting and to the colleagues and students who participated in it.

Most of the writing of this book took place while I was on a sabbatical at the National Foreign Language Center, Johns Hopkins University, Washington, DC. I am thankful to the Center and to its director, David Maxwell, for providing the facilities to work on the book. I am equally thankful to my own institution, Tel Aviv University, for providing the financial support during my sabbatical.

Yet, the most important sources of inspiration for this book, as well as for many other aspects of my life, are my two daughters, Daphna and Orlee. They are my most stimulating colleagues – always interested, curious and opinionated about issues of social and political relevance. It is from them that I generate ideas, it is with them that I share ideas, and it is for them that I am looking for answers. I often find that whatever does not pass their 'test' in our discussions is not worth researching as they provide the barometer of relevance. The discussions with Daphna and Orlee are enlightening, smart, revealing, critical and motivated by social justice and an ethical impetus to try to make this world a better place, and it is to them that, lovingly, I dedicate this book. Daphna and Orlee, in their wisdom, curiosity and enthusiasm, make such issues very meaningful. Many of the ideas in this book were generated from their schooling experiences and, hopefully, the outcomes of this book and the critical look at tests will be of benefit to other test takers.

About this book

This book is not about tests, but rather about their uses, effects and consequences. It is about how tests cannot be viewed as isolated and neutral events but rather as embedded in educational, social, political and economic contexts. Tests, therefore, need to be interpreted and understood within this complex context.

The book consists of four parts: Part I establishes the power of tests; Part II reports on empirical studies and cases relating to the use of tests; Part III interprets the results of the studies and examines their consequences, arriving at a model for the use of tests; and Part IV proposes critical agendas for democratizing and limiting the power of tests and protecting the rights of test takers.

Part I establishes the power of tests. Chapter 1 introduces the concept of 'use-oriented testing' by distinguishing it from traditional testing. In traditional testing the focus is on the accuracy of tests with little consideration for their use while 'use-oriented testing' views tests not as isolated events but rather as embedded in social, educational and political contexts. It therefore considers how tests are used in society and the nature of their consequences to different stakeholders.

Chapter 2 echoes the voices of test takers about their perceptions, views about and attitudes towards tests and the testing experiences, as it is from test takers that one can learn most about how tests are used. The quotes provided by test takers demonstrate that tests are used in ways that are frightening, deterring and controlling. Tests create fear, anxiety and subversion in test takers, leading them to develop strategies to comply with the demands of the tests.

Chapter 3 interprets the reactions of test takers within a framework of the powerful uses of tests. It claims that (a) tests lead to detrimental effects for individual test takers and others affected by their results and (b) tests are used as disciplinary tools by those in authority, enticing test takers to change their behaviour along the demands of tests in order to maximize their score.

Chapter 4 describes the built-in features that tests possess that allow such uses. These features include the use of the language of numbers and science, 'objective' type items and the use of tests by powerful institutions.

Chapter 5 describes the process by which tests emerged from tools originally aimed at democratizing education to instruments used by government and other agencies as arms for policy making and for perpetuating elites – a phenomenon which is especially noticeable with high-stake tests and in countries with centralized educational systems.

Chapter 6 describes the temptations of those in authority to use tests for policy making and for affecting the behaviour of test takers. It attempts to understand what makes tests attractive to decision makers. It shows that tests enjoy the widespread trust of the public, are considered efficient and cheap ways of making policy, are means to dominate without being challenged, have great visibility and provide bureaucrats with evidence of actions.

Given the power of tests, Part II examines how this power is exercised in actual language testing situations. It reports on three empirical studies and a number of cases which examined systematically the uses of tests focusing on two dimensions – the intentions of decision makers in introducing tests and the effects that these tests had on education and society. Four of the five chapters in this part present empirical studies and cases, and one chapter provides background on the intentions and effects of tests.

Chapter 7 defines two domains of inquiry with regard to the uses of tests: the intentions behind using tests and their effects. It then reviews the literature for each of the domains.

Chapters 8 to 10 describe research studies that examined the effects and consequences of three language tests – a reading comprehension test (Chapter 8), an Arabic test (Chapter 9) and an English as a second language test (Chapter 10) – all showing how tests serve as tools for policy making, as can be learned both from the intentions and the effects.

Chapter 11 reports on specific cases where the power of tests are exercised in education and the political arena. In these situations tests are used for purposes such as gate-keeping, selection, ethnic cleansing, controlling and defining knowledge, and limiting entrance of immigrants and potential citizens.

Part III draws conclusions from the studies and cases and interprets the findings in a broader perspective. It consists of four chapters that draw conclusions and provides theoretical interpretations as to the uses of tests.

Chapter 12 draws conclusions from the studies and cases focusing on intentions and effects, showing how tests are used by authorities as a means of introducing personal policies and agendas. These uses lead to a complex pattern of effects such as redefining and imposing language knowledge. The chapter also shows the scant connection between intentions and effects, so that effects can seldom be predicted accurately from intentions.

Chapter 13 proposes a model of the use of tests which attempts to synthesize the findings and explain the process by which the power of tests is exercised. It explains how and why it causes test takers to change their behaviour and comply with the demands of the tests, and how those in authority, aware of this phenomenon, will introduce tests in order to create behavioural changes suited to their agendas.

Chapter 14 analyses the consequences of such uses of tests, including the redefining of knowledge, creating parallel forms of education, controlling learning, engaging in unethical behaviour, and creating covert policies and unmonitored powers. This is even more powerful with regard to language tests (especially of English) as it combines the power of language with the power of tests.

Chapter 15 contextualizes the power of tests within the notion of symbolic and ideological power, as discussed by Bourdieu (1991). It argues that symbolic power is derived from an unwritten contract between those in authority and the subjects of power who are willing to be dominated by tests, as tests serve to perpetuate their domination and provide them with a symbol of social order. The various mechanisms used to promote symbolic power are described along with the rhetorics and discoursal myths which portray tests as an ideology.

Part IV proposes strategies and solutions for minimizing and controlling the unchallenged power of tests by introducing democratic dimensions. It is the acceptance of tests as instruments which are not neutral but rather are used for controlling and introducing agendas, and that demand a response to control their power and limit their harmful consequences. Each of the four chapters addresses a different dimension of minimizing and controlling the power of tests.

The principles of 'critical language testing' are introduced in Chapter 16. These principles aim at critiquing the uses of tests, question and examine their uses, the values and beliefs inherent in them, to monitor and minimize their power and point out misuses in reference to social, ethical, educational and political contexts.

Chapter 17 introduces assessment models which are based on democratic principles of shared power, equal partnership and dialogical interactions of tester, test taker and other stakeholders. These include alternative assessment models, shared discourse and constructive and interpretive approaches.

The social and ethical responsibilities of the language tester are discussed in Chapter 18, which examines (a) the identity of the language tester and (b) his or her social responsibilities in terms of morality, ethicality and professionalism. Should the tester be a bystander in that process or is his or her role to guard against misuses, expose them or even impose sanctions?

Chapter 19 examines ways by which test takers can protect themselves from the powerful tests by discussing the rights of test takers and guards against misuses. Examples of codes of ethics are also included.

Chapter 20 is an epilogue which elaborates on the dilemmas and conflicts regarding the future of tests in light of society's competing forces and ideologies; the future of testing is then discussed in relation to these competing forces.

Acknowledgements

The Publishers are grateful to the following to reproduce copyright material:

International Language Testing Association for the 'ILTA Code of Ethics', 2000 © ILTA.

General editor's preface

There is nothing so powerful as an idea whose time has come, even if the coming was rather more protracted than several, including the author of this volume and the General Editor of this series, might ideally have wished. 'Fancy, X', Terry Quinn apparently said once, 'he works in language testing and he doesn't realise he's involved in a political activity'. Well, the best that one might say, on reading this trenchant argument by Elana Shohamy in this most recent book in the *Language in Social Series* was that the X's naivete was and still is pervasive, and, to be honest, perhaps a touch contrived. Partly encouraged of course, because the fact that any assessment has by its nature to be sponsored by authority and therefore inherently subject to policy is not something trumpeted about, partly because a discipline in which psychometric analysis must be so significant makes numbers easy to hide behind, and partly because the machinery of test design and the necessary confidentiality of its processes created a world in which the technicians were removed from the consumers, and any feedback was, at best, mediated by a range of diluting, not to say, obfuscating, procedures.

We have, it must be said, been here before, in other circumstances, other disciplines, other times. Michael Frayn's scientists' debates in his play *Copenhagen* have nothing on this, one might say. Still, those of us who were at the featured Colloquium on the topic of ethics in language testing at the AILA World Congress in Jyvaskyla in 1996, or heard the author of this book come out strongly on the topic in March 1997 at the *American Applied Linguistics Association* (AAAL) meeting, had to feel the electricity. Something was stirring in the world of testing and assessment. Since then, it has been all downhill. Special Issues of the profession's journal *Language Testing*, a (re)discovery and pronouncement of the need for professional ethics, convincing research studies on bias in benchmarking criteria, breast-beating debates on the placing of responsibilities, memorial lectures invoking the great spirit of Messick, social constructivists and psychometricians struggling in the gatherings of the *International Language Testing Association* (ILTA),

Codes of Practice, 'clean-air-type' advertisements, holier-than-thou pro-nouncements – mostly all grounded in good housekeeping concern.

The issues could not be more significant, nor so problematic, and that is why this long-awaited book carries such importance. It should be read by everyone and not, repeat not, just by language testers. It affects in particular those taking tests, and ought to affect all those administering them. The book has a strong argument to put, even an axe to grind, but it does this not by some loose and empty polemic, but by the careful setting out of the issues by an expert researcher and committed practitioner, grounded in an under-standing of language from a social theoretical perspective, and firmly an-chored in actual cases whose immediacy, relevance and authority would be hard to deny. The book is not, as I say, only directed at the language testing community or the wider audience of those involved in taking and admin-istering such tests. It addresses testing in all subjects, and its issues touch other discourse communities whose public actions and public policies have, perhaps latterly, but nevertheless have had to engage with issues of ethicality. We may think of the contexts of the law, of healthcare, of correction, of the military, and, within the academy, of science and anthropology, and more broadly still, of education as a whole. Indeed, for the whole community of applied linguistics the book has a telling relevance, since the mediating tools of such political actions, and the mediating tools of such appeals to ethics and morality, are essentially linguistic – or rather, discursive. In that sense, all involved professionally with matters of language and social action – in short, all applied linguists – need to read what Elana Shohamy sets out in *The Power of Tests*. As Tim McNamara reminds us in his survey article in the *Annual Review of Applied Linguistics* 18 (1998), and invoking Foucault's highly relevant book *Discipline and Punish: The Birth of the Prison* (Foucault, 1977), (as does the author), testing is '*the primary disciplinary site in applied linguistics*'.

Let me try to outline briefly some of the matters that are at issue in this debate. Beginning test-internally, at base they have to do with the position one takes on the nature of language, and, in particular, the extent to which the meaning potential of utterances can be circumscribed so that their nec-essary negotiability can be made amenable to valid and reliable assessment. What is clear is that any assessment of language necessarily impoverishes one's understanding of the nature of language as communication. To meet the criteria necessarily imposed by any system-wide administration of the evaluation of linguistic ability, testing and assessment have to work with a reduced understanding of language. That is the first power of a language test. It circumscribes its construct. All measures of reliability and validation are intent on seeking to reduce the essential inappropriateness of such cir-cumscription. However, just as in the case of language itself, all such meas-ures essentially imbricate particular values about what language is and what meanings are to be derived. In this, Messick could not have been more right. There can be no value-free exercise of scientific knowledge, since both that knowledge and its application are subject to opinion and belief. Language testing 'facts' are not opals in the desert. They do not glimmer waiting to be uncovered. They may be searched for, but they are constructed by agency. No test constructs are value-free, and all are indirect. As McNamara reminds us, all that tests do is to gather evidence upon which inferences are drawn about the unobservable. (McNamara, 1999).

Thus, the second power of tests lies in the control they exert over the relative admissibility of those measures and constructs whose task it is to reduce the arbitrariness of the exercise of value. In principle, we are talking here about the validation of validity. Here this book makes two important contributions. Firstly, it shifts our focus from seeing tests and testing in some monolithic sense, and argues that we should differentiate among the various steps in the cycle of test design, test validation, test delivery and test outcomes, and see each as having its own *critical moments* requiring constant scrutiny and review. Each such step has its own contexts and suggests its own participant responsibilities, and these are not uniform or identical. Moreover, such steps are implicationally related, in that, for example, challenges to one aspect of validity necessarily impinge on other areas for which validation is sought. Secondly, what it does is to shift our focus in this regard from test-internal issues (which continue, of course, to be objects and processes requiring the keenest of scrutiny) to test-external issues of effect and consequence. It is here, as Messick rightly indicated, and Shohamy has as a central tenet, that testing has to come to grips with consequential validity, that is the consequences of how scores are interpreted and tests are 'used'. Alderson once asked whether there was life after the test. Just so, and the nature of that 'life' is what is at issue here. Traditionally, the focus has been on in-house educational consequences in terms of effects on instruction, on learning, on educational advancement. With this book, and under the impact of the critical language testing *movimento*, issues of wider social concern are now on the agenda – issues of access to human rights, issues of access to the movement of peoples, issues of access to scarce resources, issues surrounding social gatekeeping, and issues of the definition of knowledge more generally.

It is here that we discern the third power of tests. Here the power is not Gramsci's coercive civil power, *egemonia* of the barrel-of-a-gun variety, more the insidious *consensual* power, akin to Foucault's capillary power, or Bourdieu's symbolic power, whereby the powerful and authoritarian captivate and incorporate the less-than-powerful into an acceptance, and indeed support, for particular modes of action, with a consequent ignoring or downplaying of alternative or critical positions. It is this exercise of consensual power that has traditionally achieved its greatest effect on approaches to testing and on the uses made of tests, as Elana Shohamy makes unmistakeably plain, in what is perhaps the most original and remarkable sections of her book. The very attractiveness of testing to those in authority as a means of determining policy and action, and the ready willingness of those most affected to subscribe to such application and use, evidences this powerful consensual effect.

Notwithstanding the fact that testers have concentrated, perfectly properly in one professional sense, on the test-internal issues of ensuring reliability and validity, and even though they have made considerable and remarkable advances especially in the improving the reliability and validity of rater judgements, and in systematically seeking the views of test-takers, it still remains true that there has been less of an engagement with this issue of effects and consequences, with hearing the voices of others outside the community, and with the social and policy context of assessment more generally. In part this is due to the demands and constraining conditions set on testers by the sources of testing sponsorship, in part because of the way that the exercise of such consensual power is typically mediated through the actions of representatives, of middlemen, and is not necessarily directly contingent on the actions of originators. This makes the issue of responsibility harder to locate, of course, as Alan Davies puts it in raising the question whether language testers should be responsible for decisions beyond test construction (Davies, 1997b), and harder to define in relation to the competing demands of its underlying, and distinct, constructs of accountability and ethics. Nonetheless, it is hard to argue against the contention that some testers have willingly or unwillingly, played into the hands of those exercisers of consensual power, and in some cases, actively conspired to extend its scope.

As recent commentators have noted, this contention raises for some the question of morality, in particular what the relationship might be between one's individual morality and that attributed to the professional community of which one is a member. On this issue, Shohamy takes, I believe, the sensible course. Rather than using the case of language testing as an occasion for some philosophical debate on universalist versus relativist positions on ethics or, worse, for some quasi-religious searching by troubled souls in quest of shriving, she sets out the case for an alternative approach to testing practice. Central to this is the construct of *critique*. By this is meant, following parallel arguments in critical discourse analysis (Fairclough, 1992), a commitment to making language testing reflexive and aware of the social and historical conditions within which a particular call for testing arises, testing is designed and administered, and the special interests and purposes of the communities and organisations it is deemed, or comes to serve; a thorough and continuing accounting of testing as a social and disciplinary practice in the light of such conditions; and a consideration of issues of equity at all stages of the testing cycle and the testing process.

On such a critical base, an alternative approach to testing can be designed, one which does not fail to engage with the struggles between practicality and desirability, and one which takes the difficult path of accountability both to ethics and morality, and to the interests of stakeholders, as its governing principle. One which, given the mutability and negotiability of language, can and must afford a certain relativity in relation to its contexts of administration and use. One which is characteristically professional in establishing Codes of Practice – admirable examples of which are provided in this book – Codes, however, which do not fudge and prevaricate on central principles, and are open to review. Now such a critical agenda is easy to set out. Many will indeed applaud. What will count, though, in language testing as in applied linguistics more generally, is what can be done. In her final chapter, Shohamy is icy cold on this issue of delivery.

Let me disclose some biography. I am not professionally a language tester, but I have been involved, at times over the last 25 years, chairing and directing the Test Development Committees of three very high stakes tests associated with either national immigration or with professional admissibility to membership, and with one international test directed at tertiary level entry. I can in consequence write with some experience of these issues. While no-one would claim, least of all me, that in all these cases, at all times, the highest standards expected of Dr Shohamy's welcome new agenda were, or perhaps, could have been achieved, they nevertheless remain, in my view, to a very large extent attainable. What does that attainability require? Firstly, language testing, like any testing, has to recognise its own fallibility and set accountability as the primary objective of the exercise. Secondly, and in support of this, it requires the systematic, continuing, organised and welcomed participation of the stakeholders. Thirdly, it deserves, and must insist on the application of the most highly developed technical expertise that can be marshalled, especially in the matter of the design of test content and in guaranteeing rater reliability. Fourthly, it requires the consistent and confrontational display of alternative evidence. Fifthly, like Caesar's slave, it needs the presence of a continuing voice which asks 'what are the consequences of this action?'.

In advancing all these desiderata (and readers will suggest others), however, we need to guard against two dangers. The first is the defeatist belief that such attainability is a chimera and that for various reasons of expediency, nothing can, or should be done. One example of this debilitating argument is the one that holds that because it may appear that we cannot control for all the social consequences of testing, nothing which is external to the test design and administration should be taken into account and attempted. In my experience, it is possible in large measure to factor such consequences, especially how test interpretations are arrived at, quite deliberately and consequentially into the practices of test design and administration, and I know that this can be, how it can be, and how it has been done. The other danger is to assume that the sponsors of tests and other stakeholders, the consumers of test results and the testees themselves, are not open to convincing debate. Here, however, testers will have to take on an unaccustomed public relational role. They will have to expound their case, and often in the public arena. They will have to learn that there is no refuge in the arcane. They will have to come up against those most affected by testing decisions in the immediacy of public and private meetings, confront their challenges, and offer their arguments. To be equipped for this, they will have to experience a wider, more socially and social-psychologically grounded training than that provided in a comfortably neutral psychometry. They will have to give muscle to their own Codes of Practice because they will come to realise that such Codes are not there just to constrain potential malpractice but to offer an actual ground for defence against those who would charge them with unprincipled practices. Why should they attempt this? How could they be a profession if they did not? How could they be concerned scholars if they did not? And if they do not, then they will need to be compelled to, and litigation will provide the cane. Having cultivated an 'ethical milieu' (Davies, 1997b) will be a start, but it will rapidly turn out not to be enough.

This critical, at times impassioned, and immensely convincing book sets out the reasons and points a way to achieving this wider accountability. It will be for the testing community to make the alternative modes of assessment and assessment practices work. It will be for the stakeholders and consumers to hold them to the bargain. Who guards the guards themselves? Ever an interesting question. Applied linguistics in action, you might say.

References

A. Davies (1997a) Introduction: the limits of ethics in language testing. *Language Testing*, 14

A. Davies (1997b) Demands of being professional in language testing. *Language Testing* 14

N.L. Fairclough (1992) *Critical language awareness.* London. Longman

M. Foucault (1977) *Discipline and punish: the birth of the prison.* Harmondsworth. Penguin

T. McNamara (1998) Policy and social considerations in language assessment. *Annual Review of Applied Linguistics* (Vol. 18 (304–319)) Cambridge. Cambridge University Press

T. McNamara (1999) *Validity in language testing: the challenge of Sam Messick's legacy.* Messick Memorial Lecture. Language Testing Research Colloquium. Tsukuba, Japan (July)

Christopher N. Candlin
General Editor,
City University of Hong Kong

I

The power of tests

Traditional testing focuses on the quality of tests, following accepted models and procedures for maximizing the accuracy of tests. Yet, very little attention is given to how tests are used, their importance in the lives of test takers and their place in society. Traditional testing does not pay much attention to the testing experience, or to the meanings and feelings that tests evoke in test takers. However, by listening to the voices of test takers it is possible to obtain evidence of the power of tests and the detrimental decisions they lead to for test takers. The use of tests as disciplinary tools by those in authority causes test takers to fear tests but at the same time to obey their rules.

What are the special features that tests possess that legitimize their power and influence? How did an instrument intended to democratize and provide equal opportunities turn into a threatening device? What features of tests tempt those in authority to use them for policy making? How did tests emerge as tools used for policy making? These are some of the topics that will be addressed in Part I of this book in an attempt to establish the dimensions of the power of tests.

1

'Use-oriented' testing

Traditional testing

Traditional testing is a scientific field, with precise boundaries and criteria. It consists of a well-defined and systematic body of knowledge. Its main focus and purpose is the creation of quality tests that can accurately measure the knowledge of those tested. Results obtained from tests are used for comparing scores of test takers, classifying test takers into appropriate proficiency levels, assigning grades and accepting or rejecting test takers. Tests, therefore, need to be of high quality and follow the careful rules of the science of psychometrics.

Testing is therefore a professional field with strict rules and applications as to what constitutes appropriate practice. High-quality tests are expected to provide the users with precise answers as to the knowledge being measured. It employs a variety of techniques for developing high-quality test items and tasks, most often of the objective mode. Its body of knowledge includes topics such as methods for computing different types of reliability (i.e. how accurate test scores are), obtaining evidence of validity (i.e. the extent to which tests measure what they are expected to measure) and procedures for examining the quality of items and tasks (i.e. the extent to which test items and tasks measure the content being tested).

Traditional testing has relied mostly on objective type items, as these minimize statistical unreliability. It rarely deviates from this as the model seems safe. While other testing methods, such as summaries, reports, and role plays, are becoming widely used, they are often accompanied by cautionary advice regarding their accuracy (Nitko, 1996). Even the uses of now popular procedures such as portfolios, self-assessment and peer assessment require that these procedures be subject to criteria judgements typical of objective testing. Only if, and when, such procedures demonstrate that they possess the 'traditional' psychometric properties can they be accepted as legitimate 'members' of the 'traditional testing club'.

In traditional testing the focus is primarily on the test; the test taker is important only as a means for examining the quality of the test. The only time the test taker is mentioned is in discussing the difficulty, discrimination and other indices so that 'good' test takers get items right while the 'bad' ones get them wrong. 'Good' and 'bad' are generally defined by the performance on the test being examined. Rarely are there any investigations or discussions as to the sources, causes and reasons that make test items good or bad, easy or difficult. Is it that the teaching that preceded the test was ineffective, that the material tested was too difficult, that the test taker was absent from class when the material had been taught, or that the test items required cognitive processing that the test taker did not possess? The general rule is that the test takers need to match their performances to the tests rather than the tests to the test takers.

Traditional testing, then, is not interested in test use. Once the test is designed and developed, its items written and administered, its format piloted, items and statistics computed, reliability calculated and evidence of validity obtained, the role of the tester is complete. The task ends when psychometrically sound results are satisfactorily achieved. This is the point at which the test is being delivered to those who contracted it and is ready to be used with 'real life' people, the test takers.

Thus, traditional testing is not interested in the motives for introducing tests, in the intentions and rationale for using tests or in the examinations of whether intentions were fulfilled. It is not interested in the steps taken in preparation for tests or in how test takers feel about tests. It is especially not interested in the consequences of tests and their effects on those who failed or succeeded in them. It also overlooks how the test affected knowledge, learning patterns and habits. Traditional testing views tests as isolated events, detached from people, society, motives, intentions, uses, impacts, effects and consequences.

'Use-oriented' testing

'Use-oriented' testing views testing as embedded in educational, social and political contexts. It addresses issues related to the rationale for giving tests and the effects that tests have on test takers, education and society. It is concerned with what happens to the test takers who take the tests, the knowledge that is created by tests, the teachers who prepare for the tests, the materials and methods used for tests, the decisions to introduce tests, the uses of the results of tests, the parents whose children are subject to the tests, the ethicality and fairness of the tests, and the long- and short-term consequences that tests have on education and society.

In examining the use of tests, attention is given to the reasons and intentions for introducing tests, to the test takers who take the tests, to the teachers who teach for tests, to the students who practise for the tests, to the knowledge created by tests, to ethical and fair behaviours of tests, to the rationale for introducing tests, to the educational systems where tests are used, and to the effects and consequences that tests have on education and society.

There is also a realization that while testers are busy creating 'the perfect' tests, these tests are often used for purposes other than those for which they were intended. This is especially noted with regard to commercial enterprises, government agencies and organizations that use tests in ways which some would consider to be unethical. There is therefore a growing awareness of the need to examine tests from broader and more expanded perspectives consisting of various dimensions of the use of tests.

While for many years professionalism in testing meant the development of high-quality tests that pass accuracy criteria, some testers are realizing that it is not enough, as tests cannot be viewed as neutral instruments. There is therefore a growing concern about the power of tests and their uses in society.

In the field of testing, issues about the use of tests – i.e. intentions, effects and consequences – were considered to be external to traditional testing but there has recently been a renewed interest in this topic. Messick (1981, 1989, 1994, 1996), for example, claims that tests embody values that too often are unrecognized and unexamined, as they are connected to psychological, social and political variables that have effects on curriculum, ethicality, social classes, bureaucracy, politics and knowledge. He, therefore, emphasized the need to study aspects related to the consequences of tests and noted that such aspects should be considered as part of a broader definition of validity, as they involve questions of values and consequences of score interpretation and test use:

> The consequential aspect of construct validity includes evidence and rationale for evaluating the intended and unintended consequences of score interpretation and use in both the short and long term, especially those associated with bias in scoring and interpretation, with unfairness in test use, and with positive or negative washback effects on teaching and learning.

> (Messick, 1994: 251)

Gipps (1994) interprets this phenomenon by claiming that testing is experiencing a shift from a purely technical perspective to a test-use perspective.

In the field of language testing as well, testers have begun to show a growing interest in the roles that language tests play in society. Spolsky (1998) argues that rather than putting all the effort into building more and more reliable measures of less and less important elements of language proficiency, testers should support the study of the meaning and use of the inaccurate measures they already have. Testers, he notes, should accept the inevitable uncertainty of tests and turn their attention to the ways in which tests are used.

As a result, language testers have begun to address various issues of test use[1] focusing on topics of test ethicality, test bias, the effect and impact of tests on teaching and learning, and the use of tests. Additional topics are the extent to which language tests define linguistic knowledge, determine membership, classify people and stipulate criteria for success and failure of individual test takers. These are some of the topics that will be addressed and discussed in the following chapters.

Note

1. See *Language Testing*, 13 (3), 1996; *Language Testing*, 14 (4), 1997; conference in Carleton University, Summer 1998, and the theme of the Language Testing Research Colloquium, Tskuba, Japan, 1999.

2

Voices of test takers

It is probably not possible to find a person in the modern world who did not go through a testing experience at least once in his or her lifetime. It is difficult to find a person who does not have a testing story that relates to how a single test affected and changed his or her life, for good or for bad. The experiences of taking tests are remembered by test takers for many years after the events have taken place. It is through the voices of test takers who report on the testing experiences and their consequences that the features of the use of tests can be identified.

Yet, in the testing literature test takers are often kept silent; their personal experiences are not heard or shared. It seems that the testing profession – those who produce tests – are not interested in such accounts. However, as will be noted in this chapter, listening to the voices of test takers can provide testers with a new and unique perspective and a deep insight into tests and their meanings.

Personal accounts

The excerpts given below represent a sample of some personal accounts of what testers say and feel about tests.

A death wish

In the following poem the Irish novelist J. McGahern (1977, quoted in Madaus, 1990) describes the impact that tests have on a child who is about to take a test:

> *Please God may I not fail*
> *Please God may I get over sixty per cent*
> *Please God may I get a high place*
> *Please God may all those likely to beat*
> *me get killed in road accidents and*
> *may they die roaring.*

This poem shows how fearful test takers are of failing tests and how detrimental the experience is for them. They clearly feel a lack of control, as succeeding on a test is like 'an act of God'. They pray to pass the test in the same way as they pray to be saved from a terrible disaster or an awful danger. Further, doing well on tests implies that every peer is in competition; friends turn into enemies and rivals in the high-stake race where the only survival strategy is the elimination of the competitors. The poem also shows how central tests are in one's life and the high price that test takers are willing to pay in order to succeed.

Causing deterioration in one's life

On a memorable night in a bar named Dingo in Arnheim, the Netherlands, during a conference on language testing, my friend and colleague Tim McNamara and myself found ourselves deeply engaged in a conversation with a drug junkie. Upon asking what brought him to this low point in his life he told us a long story about what started it all. He recalled the traumatic event of taking a standardized test in 7th grade and failing it badly. His failure was such a disappointment for his father, a university literature professor, that from that point on his father started rejecting him. This eventually led to a series of events that turned our conversation partner into an outcast in his family leading him to leave home and gradually reach the point where he is at now. Needless to say we felt responsible, a face-to-face encounter with one of 'our own' victims . . .

Whether the story told is an accurate account of the events or whether the test was used as a pretext, is not the main point of the story. It is important, though, that the story reflects the perception of a person about a single event, a high-stake test, that had a detrimental effect on his life. The specific event – failure on a standardized test – is perceived as connected and as responsible for a number of additional events, contexts and consequences. In this case a failure on a test evoked rejections from a family, low self-esteem and self-worth, a general negative attitude towards life to the point of criminal behaviour. It points to a phenomenon whereby the results of a test get out of control. It shows how a single event is so central that it becomes accountable and is perceived as responsible for future behaviour and events.

Forcing into a profession

This is a story of a person who was wondering about her life possibilities and therefore decided to examine her opportunities and talents by taking a number of tests in different areas. Little did she know that the exceptionally high scores she received on one of the tests would lead representatives of a secret agency to wait at her doorstep and attempt to recruit her to the

Canadian secret service. They claimed that her high scores on the test convinced them, without any doubt, that she was an unusually appropriate candidate with exceptional talents for a specific job in the service. They would offer her high sums of money if she would join. She described how difficult, almost impossible, it had been for her to convince the agents that she had no interest whatsoever in 'joining the forces' and in taking such a job. She was also surprised how they could deduce her exceptional talents and capabilities based on her performance on a single test. She eventually was able to get out of the offer while learning a lesson about the risks of 'taking tests, just for fun'.

In this example, again, the performance on one single test has the potential of affecting other events for better or for worse. It provides further evidence of the blind trust that users of tests have in test scores, believing that tests can provide valid predictions and indications of all kind of performances, especially for high-status and responsible jobs. It can be compared to the trust in fortune tellers possessing supernatural powers of predicting the future. The example further shows how powerful the owners of the testing information are in relation to the powerlessness of test takers.

Stigmatizing people as failures

On June 12th, 1991 an article reporting on the administration of a national test in reading comprehension appeared in the Israeli newspaper *Haaretz*. The article described some of the consequences of administering a high stake test in one school. Specifically, there were a number of interviews with children who were not allowed to participate in the test which took place in their school. The reason given by the principal was the concern that their participation would lower the average score of the school. Instead, the article reports, they were sent to the gym to watch a movie. The article provides a close insight into their feelings of humility and shame as the non-participation perpetuated their feelings of failure and contributed to their low self-esteem. The article also contains another detail about a bright student who asked to be absent from the school for personal reasons the day the test was to be administered. However, he could not obtain permission from the principal to leave for fear that his absence would lower the average score of the school.

This article points to the strong power and authority of tests in the life of schools and demonstrates the high price educators (in this case the principal) are willing to pay schools succeed on tests. It is clear to the principal that performance on the test is the major (and often the single) criterion for judging the quality of the school. The high-stake test is so important that it leads the principal to become engaged in the unethical behaviour of lying, humiliating students, violating rules as well as damaging the validity of the test scores. It further indicates that the principal is very aware of the high-stake status and its eventual consequences for the school. The high price is also paid by the students whose perceptions of failure are perpetuated in their own eyes as well as in the eyes of their parents, teachers and peers.

Whatever will be will be

I am an English teacher at the secondary level. I teach students who must take a standardized test in their final year of secondary school. I tell my students these stories from my own experience in order to remind them that failing a test does not necessarily lead to death. (This was a lesson I had to learn because I was usually quite successful on tests, which made me fear the results of failure.)

In grade 11 Physics, as the year progressed I felt more and more alienated. I attributed this to the teacher's use of multiple-choice tests. By the final exam, I perceived no connection between what I studied and what I was tested on, or how. When I looked at the exam (on the day of the exam) I was sure I had no idea of how to proceed. So my response was to make up a little song 'in my head', and I silently sang it to myself 'a a b ccc d a . . .' and so on. I failed the exam, but not by much. I got about 43 per cent. I passed Physics, barely. I did not die, but you sure do not want me to build you a bridge.

From the above it is obvious how fearful and threatened test takers are of tests, as success is perceived as 'pure luck' and has little to do with true knowledge. There is a feeling that the test and the test takers are in the control of the tester. In terms of knowledge of the topic tested, performance on the test is not viewed as an indication of actual knowledge. Thus the test taker is at the mercy of the tester who has his or her own agenda on what should be included in a test. The consequences are that, in this 'testing game', guessing and luck are the main strategies that test takers are left with in order to survive the test's demands. Test takers therefore develop a variety of gimmicks, tactics and tricks in order to pass the test and gain the benefits associated with its results.

The choice between life and passing a test

This is the story of my driving tests. I did not pass the first time because I was distracted by a driver-tester trainee. The trainee in the back seat made me nervous when she would practically lie down when I shoulder checked. During my second attempt, an old man stumbled through an intersection while I had a green light. The tester yelled, 'The light is green. You should be proceeding through the intersection!' I had to stop so as not to hit the man. I yelled back 'Just because the light is green is not a good enough reason to die!' I failed the second test, and the stated reason was 'Stops at green light'. I passed my third test in a blizzard. I have never had an accident, or even a ticket.

The above indicates that success on a test is detached from reality, from rights and wrongs. Test takers learn that in the testing game there are rules to follow, even if they are not rational and make no sense. Test takers know that the best strategy for a tester is to comply with and follow the testing rules – no questions asked. They learn very early that harsh consequences may result from not following the testing rules – in the above case, it was denial of the permission to drive. Yet, test takers frequently face situations when difficult and complex ethical dilemmas need to be resolved with no easy solutions, as disagreeing with the test's demands is something that test takers have no right to do.

Brilliance does not always pay

When I was in grade 8 in a small community outside of Burlington, Ontario, our school introduced a standard IQ test. Well, this was a new and special event – at a time long before many people came to understand that tests may not be all they are cracked up to be. Actually the views about tests paralleled the wisdom of the time on smoking cigarettes. I specifically remember one TV ad which showed a doctor in a white lab coat drawing heavily on a KOOLS cigarette and, as he inhaled deeply and exhaled with satisfaction, he fixed his gaze wonderingly/lovingly on the cigarette itself and announced to the viewers: 'KOOLS – it's like a breath of fresh air'. Anyway, back to the story. As I said I lived in a small community which had a local elementary school of a few hundred students – it was a predominantly working-class middle-class melange with academic achievement being only so so important. This is in contrast to my family where doing well in school and being 'smart' were simply what Jews did – at least as my parents saw it. So I was a particularly successful student in a rather non-academic environment which in part perhaps accounted for my intellectual successes and arrogance. This background is important as it frames my attitude towards the test we were being asked to take. I went into the exam almost gleefully – sure that this would be one more attestation to my brilliance. I was the first one finished – which came as no surprise to me, and home I went. The following day the principal called me into his office to talk about the test results. What he said to me was the following: 'Barbara, you have to open the test!' I had completed the front and back pages and hadn't realized it had a substantial middle part. No wonder I finished so quickly! Now to make matters more messy, the principal allowed me to complete the test in his office. Imagine, had I been a weak student – how this behaviour would have been clear proof of my stupidity. Now perhaps in this small school, this particular principal would have given the same opportunity to any student, given that the test was new, etc., etc. I have never been sure and have been sceptical on one-shot test results ever since . . .

The above indicates how easy it is to fail on a test for the wrong reasons. Failing on a test is often not related to the topic tested; in this case it was for not following the test's instructions. In examining the score of the test it is often not possible to trace the reasons for the failure. Yet, as the above case indicates, the cost for misunderstanding is significantly greater for low-level students as it perpetuates their low standing. High-level test takers, on the other hand, often have additional opportunities to demonstrate their competencies, as failure on one testing occasion is perceived as an exception to their generally high performance.

Test takers' views about classroom tests

Below are additional statements provided by test takers that point to their perceptions and views about classroom tests. These statements were obtained from questionnaires that asked secondary school students to express their attitudes towards classroom language tests (Shohamy, 1985).

We spent ten lessons conjugating the past tense but on the test there were only two conjugations.

I never learn anything from tests because the teacher never corrects the mistakes I make, so I end up at the same place where I was before I took the test, except now I also have a bad grade.

I don't believe that a test is a good measure of my performance, let alone on a day when I do not feel well.

I don't see the connection between the test and my knowledge, otherwise, how can I explain the fact that I get good grades on English tests, but last week when I met an American, I could not say anything in English? How come we are never asked to speak on tests?

Our teacher uses the test as a punishment; whenever we don't behave she tells us we will have a test the following day. Sometimes she even asks us to take out a sheet of paper and write the test on the spot.

A test really makes me study, I would have never opened a book if it weren't for the test. I think the pressure is good for me.

I hate to flunk; tests always show me that I am a failure.

It seems that whenever the teacher is unprepared she asks us to write a test.

I don't mind the test, what I do mind is that it takes the teacher such a long time to correct it. By the time I get it back, I forget what it was all about.

I think it is really strange that whenever I study hard, I don't get a good grade but when I don't study at all, I happen to succeed. Does it say something about me or about the test?

What I hate most is when the teacher does not tell us in advance what the test will cover. It seems that I am always studying the wrong things.

Why do we need tests? The teacher knows how well we are doing anyway.

These statements reveal similar phenomena with regard to classroom tests as were expressed in the narratives. Test takers have low trust in classroom tests and view them as procedures which are not indicative of their real language knowledge. They do not view tests as useful tools for learning and note that tests are detached from 'real life' knowledge and performance. Test takers believe that classroom tests do not necessarily serve as educational tools but they often serve other purposes. Teachers tend to use tests as punishments, for control, for filling time when they are not prepared and for creating discipline. Test takers view tests as detached from real learning, as success on tests is often dependent on luck. Students often feel that classroom tests are useless in the classroom context, as they believe that teachers know how well they are doing based on a variety of other classroom performances. At the same time, though, test takers confess that tests do have the role of creating pressure and motivating them to study, mostly out of fear of their consequences.

Conclusions

The personal experiences and reactions of test takers towards tests, as reported in this chapter, provide convincing evidence of the centrality of tests in the lives of test takers. They point out the negative attitudes that test takers have towards tests, as expressed in the fear and low trust they have in test results. Test takers are threatened by tests as they view them as powerful, authoritative and leading to detrimental consequences. Test takers feel that tests are used in ways which are frightening, deterring and controlling, leading them to develop various survival strategies as they realize the radical effects that tests can have on their lives, especially given the blind trust decision makers have in the results.

While test takers perceive tests as powerful, they see themselves as power-*less*, realizing that they have as little control over the requirements to take tests as over their consequences. Since success in tests is so crucial for the test taker, they comply with the test's demands and 'play the game' in order to succeed, even to the point that they would engage in behaviours that can be considered unethical. Test takers are willing to engaged in such behaviour in spite of the low trust they have in the ability of the tests to judge their knowledge. This may explain why test takers often perceive performance on tests as 'pure luck', like a supernatural power they have no control over, with no understanding of the meaning of the results. Test takers therefore develop a cynical view about tests, and use gimmicks to help them to survive the testing experience, to enable them to have some control over this uncontrollable situation. Finally, test takers are very realistic about the consequences of the tests. Experience has taught them that these consequences go far beyond the test score and may affect a number of crucial future events, for better or for worse. Tests can affect self-esteem, confidence, pride, stigmas and opportunities.

Some of the descriptors provided by test takers are listed below:

- Threatening/frightening
- Detached from reality
- Lead to detrimental consequences
- Powerful
- Create competition
- Require survival strategies
- Have long-range effects
- Unjust/unfair
- Deterring
- Biased
- Indication of failure
- Depends on luck and supernatural powers
- Lead to unethical behaviours

This chapter has demonstrated how, by listening to test takers, it is possible to learn about the centrality of tests in test takers' lives and about the strategies test takers develop in order to overcome testing difficulties. It is certainly worth while for testers to listen to these voices as they can provide evidence on the uses of tests in education and society.

3

Powerful uses of tests

The voices of test takers, as echoed in Chapter 2, reveal that tests evoke fear, unfairness, powerlessness, injustice, deterrence, bias, suspicion, failure and antagonism. Why is it that those who experience tests develop such strong reactions? What is it that turned tests into such devices?

This chapter argues that it is the manner in which tests are used that causes test takers to react in such ways. First discussed are the detrimental effects of test results and their effects on the lives of test takers; second is the use of tests as disciplinary tools by those in authority, creating a situation whereby test takers are forced to change their behaviour in order to comply with the demands of the tests. Each of these uses of tests will now be discussed.

Tests have detrimental effects on test takers

The uses of test results have detrimental effects for test takers since such uses can create winners and losers, successes and failures, rejections and acceptances. Test scores are often the sole indicators for placing people in class levels, for granting certificates and prizes, for determining whether a person will be allowed to continue in future studies, for deciding on a profession, for entering special education classes, for participating in honour classes, for getting accepted to higher education and for obtaining jobs.

Doing well on tests can take a person to the best university and open the way to an excellent education; doing poorly can send a person to a low level university and block the possibility of higher education, resulting in poor education. Doing well on a test may grant a person a scholarship, while doing poorly implies a need to work harder. Doing well on a test may lead to a person entering a desired profession, while doing poorly may lead to an unwanted job. Doing well on a test may mean that a person is given permission to migrate to a new country and start a new life, while doing poorly may force a person to stay somewhere he or she does not wish to be. Doing well on a test may mean that a person will win a prize or a scholarship, while doing poorly may result in having to spend ample time working before he or she can afford to continue studies. Doing well on a test may mean that a person can be classified as a success, while doing poorly may mean that he or she will be classified as a failure.

Tests, then, can open or close doors, provide or take away opportunities, and in general shape the lives of individuals in many different areas. It is often the performance on a single test, often on one occasion at a single point in time, that can lead to irreversible, far-reaching and high-stake decisions. Even in situations when there is a possibility to take a test again, test takers often hesitate to do so because of the blind trust they have in the authority of test results and their own limited power. After all, tests are administered by organizations, teachers, principals and testing agencies, which are much more powerful than the individual test takers.

These detrimental effects of tests and the high-stake decisions they lead to are described by Noam (1996: 9):

> How we assess can support careers and make people successful, but it can also destroy people's careers, or at least place unfair burdens on individuals' self-perception and unnecessary hurdles in the path of their achievement.

Madaus (1990) emphasizes the fact that tests affect the rite of passage as performance on a single test often provides a powerful indicator of the future of individuals (1990: 5):

> a single standardized test score independently triggers an automatic admission, promotion, placement or graduation decision. These decisions are non-negotiable even in the act of contradictory judgments from educators about what a student knows or can do.

The detrimental effect of one specific test, the SAT (Scholastic Aptitude Test), in shaping the future of students is described by Schwartz (1999: 30):

> In a culture obsessed with measurement, the SAT has arguably become the single most important test for American high school students – an academic and psychic rite of passage that strongly influences future educational options, prompts fierce anxiety and serves as an almost mystical barometer of self-worth.

Schwartz goes on to add (1999: 31):

> The SATs are among the primary criteria for many sources of financial assistance and they have become pivotal in debates about affirmative action as well.

Thus, the use of tests to make detrimental decisions for individuals is one of their major sources of power.

Tests are used as disciplinary tools

In addition, tests are used as a method of imposing certain behaviours on those who are subject to them. Tests are capable of dictating to test takers what they need to know, what they will learn and what they will be taught. The use of tests as disciplinary tools means that test takers are forced to change their behaviour to suit the demands of the test. Tests takers are willing to do so in order to maximize their scores, given the detrimental effects the results may have on their lives, as noted earlier.

Using tests as disciplinary tools is an extension of the manipulation of tests by those in authority – policy makers, principals and teachers – into effective instruments for policy making. It is the realization that test takers will change their behaviour in order to succeed on tests that leads those in authority to use tests *to cause* a change in behaviour in accordance with certain priorities. The use of tests as disciplinary tools causes test takers to develop fear and anxiety in the face of tests as they feel they lack control – captive and at the mercy of the demands of the test.

Spolsky (1995, 1997) notes that the use of tests for disciplinary purposes is not new; historically, tests and examinations have always been used for such purposes. Since the Biblical event of the shibooleth, tests have been used for power and control. The Chinese invented the examination to provide the emperor with senior officials who would be answerable to him, not to powerful courtiers, and this served its purpose for a thousand years. The Jesuits brought the system to Europe in the seventeenth century to maintain tight control of school curricula and of the classroom (Madaus, 1990).

The use of tests for power and control is argued strongly by Foucault. In *Discipline and Punish: The Birth of the Prison* (1979) he stated that examinations have built-in features that allow them to be used for exercising power and control.[1] Tests serve as a means of observing hierarchy and normalizing judgement. They can be used for surveillance to quantify, classify and punish. Their power is that they can be used to differentiate people and to judge people. Tests consist of rituals and ceremony along with the establishment of truth, and all in the name of objectivity.

> The examination combines the technique of an observing hierarchy and those of normalizing judgment. It is a normalizing gaze, a surveillance that makes it possible to quantify, classify and punish. It establishes over individuals a visibility through which one differentiates and judges them. That is why, in all the mechanisms of discipline, the examination is highly ritualized.

In it are combined the ceremony of power and the form of the experiment, the deployment of force and the establishment of truth. At the heart of the procedures of disciplines, it manifests the subjection of those who are perceived as objects and the objectification of those who are subjected.

(Foucault, 1979: 184)

The notion that tests represent social technology is introduced by Madaus (1990) as an extension of the use of tests as disciplinary tools. He claims that tests are scientifically created tools that historically have been used as mechanisms for control and power deeply embedded in education, government and business. The test is a means of social technology as it can impose behaviours on individuals and groups and can define what students are expected to know. It therefore guarantees the movement of knowledge from the teacher to the pupil, but it extracts from the pupil a knowledge destined and reserved for the teacher.

Madaus also comments on how uncritical society is and how much faith it has in scientific and technological solutions given by tests. Tests, he notes, reflect the values of test makers, test users and policy makers, and therefore have the potential to perpetuate these in scientific and technological solutions given by tests. Test, he notes, reflect the values of test makers, test users and policy makers and therefore have the potential to perpetuate current social and educational inequalities. Madaus observes that the disciplinary role of tests is manifested through various strategies, such as test scores that enable the accumulation and aggregation of student marks, organize, rank and classify them as well as form categories, determine averages, fix norms, describe groups, compare results across units of aggregation and fix individuals and groups in a population distribution.

The power of tests to affect and define people is also expressed by Hanson (1993). He notes that tests have become social institutions in their own right, taken for granted and unquestioned. Specifically, while a testing event is only a minute representation of the whole person, tests are used both to define and produce the person, and to keep him or her powerless and under surveillance.

The role of tests as disciplinary tools goes beyond the individual test taker, and in a number of domains tests can affect whole societies. Tests can affect and manipulate educational or political systems, control curricula and redefine the knowledge of communities. At the school level, tests are used as disciplinary tools when principals use school-wide exams to drive teachers to teach or when teachers use tests and quizzes to motivate students to learn and to impose discipline. Tests can also be introduced to upgrade the status and prestige of specific topics or subjects. On political and national levels, tests are used as a means of screening populations, excluding groups from participation, ranking institutions, limiting funding, defining knowledge and gate-keeping to prevent the entry of unwanted groups.

The use of tests as disciplinary tools by political institutions is discussed by McNamara (1997) who notes that tests have become an arm of policy reform in education and vocational training as well as in immigration policy. Such policy initiatives are seen within educational systems as well as in the workforce. A concern for national standards of educational achievement in a competitive global economy, together with a heightened demand for account-ability of government expenditures, has propelled a number of initiatives involving assessment as an arm of government educational policy at national, state and district levels.

In all these situations the use of tests as disciplinary tools means that certain demands are imposed on test takers from above while they are forced into a position where they have no choice but to comply with these demands. Compliance means a change in behaviour in line with the requirements of the test. While test takers and systems tend to comply with such disciplinary demands, they also resent doing so as they feel that it is imposed on them without their voice being heard. It is the powerful uses of tests – their detrimental effects and their uses as disciplinary tools – that are responsible for the strong feelings that tests evoke in test takers, as described and dis-cussed in Chapter 2.

Note

1. It is worth noting that Foucault's biography as described in Eribon (1991) provides convincing evidence of his own experience and sufferings from tests, making him a 'test victim'. It is reported there that Foucault suffered from the consequences of tests as a disciplinary tool, causing him to fail on high-stake tests. References are made to situations when tests played detri-mental roles in his life. It is very likely that being a victim of tests led him to gain special insight into the use of tests as disciplinary tools in Western societies.

4

Features of power

Chapter 3 argued that tests have detrimental effects and, at the same time, are used as disciplinary tools. Yet tests also possess specific features that enable them to be used in such powerful ways. This chapter identifies and discusses these features.

Tests are administered by powerful institutions

One important feature that grants tests power is that they are administered by powerful institutions. This means that in an interaction between the tester and the test taker it is the tester who holds the power. After all it is the tester who makes the important decisions of what to test, how to test, how to score, and how to deliver and interpret the results. The only numbers the test taker can refer to are those provided by the tester and these can only be challenged if one has a counter number, which is generally impossible for the test taker to obtain.

Hanson (1993: 19) notes:

> In nearly all cases test givers are organizations, while test takers are individuals. Test-giving agencies use tests for the purpose of making decisions or taking actions with reference to test takers – if they are to pass a course, receive a certificate, be admitted to college, receive a fellowship, get a job or promotion. That, together with the fact that organizations are more powerful than individuals, means that the testing situation nearly always places test givers in a position of power over test takers.

Further, it is the tester who determines the information and knowledge that will be tested, and the information the test taker needs to comply with the test. It is a self-sustaining system through which the testing organization – whether it is a school, educational system, government or industry – has total non-negotiable control over the knowledge input, and can provide a mechanism for continuous control over information and power. The knowledge included in tests is determined unequally and is dictated by those who plan and write the tests. It is this knowledge that can control, monitor and block the entrance of those who are not party to it.

Tests use the language of science

Another feature that provides tests with power is their use of the language of science. The language of science in Western societies grants authority, status and power. Testing is perceived as a scientific discipline because it is experimental, statistical and uses numbers. It therefore enjoys the prestige granted to science and is viewed as objective, fair, true and trustworthy.

MacIntyre (1984) notes that the 'objective' and 'empirical' information gleaned from tests is then used by those who make decisions based on tests to support their beliefs and to win trust in their decisions. He states that since the aim of bureaucrats is to adjust means to ends in the most economical and efficient way, they will deploy scientific knowledge organized in terms of, and comprising a set of, universal law-like generalizations to help them. Schwandt (1989) elaborates on this phenomenon by claiming that bureaucratic managerial expertise in both the public and the private sector rests on this assumption of scientifically based practice. Evaluators, policy analysts, researchers and consultants enhance bureaucratic expertise by acting as scientific sources.

This phenomenon is interesting as testers know that they are unable to generate accurate generalizations concerning human behaviour, in view of the constraints imposed by real-world problems on methods of scientific investigations. Yet, at the same time, there is an unquestioned belief on the part of managers, policy makers and the public at large that the evaluator is an expert who provides scientifically derived knowledge.

Tests use the language of numbers

A similar feature that grants power to testers is the use of the language of numbers. Much has been written about the use of numbers and statistics as effective devices for power, and about the fact that numbers speak more than words (McLuhan, 1962). Like the language of science, the language of numbers is considered to be a symbol of objectivity, scientism and rationalism – all features which provide those who are affected by them with an illusion of truth, trust, legitimacy and status. The power of numbers also lies in the perception of the public that they are objective and therefore represent some 'truth', with a strong implication that they are not open for discussion and challenge. Broadfoot (1996: 86) states that

> This very objectivity, this recourse to specific rationality, lends to the assessment a legitimacy which makes it hard to refute.

The power of numbers lies in the fact they can be challenged only by using different numbers to counteract them. In testing, however, the tester has the numbers while the test taker does not, and the only numbers to which he or she can refer are those provided by the tester, who 'owns' the numbers.

Numbers are also considered powerful because they lend themselves to the classification and standardization of test takers, and thus enable test takers to be judged according to a common yardstick. Thus, when numbers are used for disseminating test results they provide decision makers with power, authority, control and legitimacy for decisions and sanctions.

Tests use written forms of communication

Both Foucault (1979) and Madaus (1990, 1994) argue that a special feature of the power of tests is the use of the written form of communication. According to Foucault the written form marked the beginning of a pedagogy that functions as a science. Foucault (1979: 21) notes that

> it is the documentation of the written examination, in combination with the quantifiable mark, that made it possible not only to objectify individuals, but also to form, describe, and objectify groups.

Madaus (1990) claims that it was not until the latter part of the eighteenth century, when paper was more readily available, that written tests were systematically introduced into the educational system. Foucault (1979) contends that earlier tests employed the oral modes and therefore left room for a dialogue between a tester and a test taker. In such situations the student had the opportunity to ask questions, elaborate on what he or she had learned, and demand clarification. The written test, on the other hand, introduced a form of discourse which altered the act of communication from a dialogue to a one-way channel of communication, focusing on what the teacher had taught without considering the test taker's views and interpretations. Thus, while the oral mode was characterized by features of negotiation, elaboration, expansion of ideas, use of contextual clues, correction, argument, revision, debate and the reading of facial clues, the written mode is one-sided. In this mode the information flows in one direction only as the test taker writes what he or she knows in response to his or her interpretations of a written stimulus. The written test defines what is expected and forces students to reveal periodically how their learning is progressing:

> it has guaranteed the movement of knowledge from the teacher to the pupil, but it extracted from the pupil a knowledge destined and reserved for the teacher.
>
> (Foucault, 1979: 187)

Tests rely on documentation

Documentation is an additional feature that enables powerful uses of tests.

> The examination that places individuals in a field of surveillance also situates them in a network of writing; it engages them in a whole mass of documents that capture and fix them. The procedures of examination were accompanied at the same time by a system of intense registration and of documentary accumulation. A 'power of writing' was constituted as an essential part in the mechanisms of discipline.
>
> (Foucault, 1979: 189)

According to Foucault, it is not only that the aptitude of each individual is being assessed, but that the procedure of writing situates these abilities and indicates the possible use that might be made of them. The procedure of writing makes it possible to integrate individual data into cumulative systems in such a way that they are not lost, and to arrange things so that an individual could be located in the general register and, conversely, each datum of the individual examination might affect overall calculations. Owing to the whole apparatus of writing that accompanied it, the examination opened up two correlative possibilities. First, the individual was redefined as a describable, analysable object. This happened not in order to reduce the individual to 'specific' features, as did naturalists in relation to other living beings, but in order to maintain the test taker in his or her individual sources, in his or her particular ovulation, and in his or her own aptitude or abilities, under the gaze of a permanent corpus of knowledge. Secondly, a comparative system was constituted that made possible the measurement of overall phenomena, the description of groups, the characterization of collective facts, the calculation of the gaps between individuals, and their distribution in a given 'population'.

Documentation, then, implies that what happens in a test is recorded, remains on record, and will provide those who are interested in the information with evidence for possible sanctions against the test takers.

Tests use objective formats

The employment of the objective format refers to the genre in which test questions are poised. Specifically, most tests used by testing agencies employ 'objective' items such as multiple choice and true–false. The assumption underlying these procedures (and the reason they are called 'objective') is that they call for one correct answer, i.e. one 'truth', one interpretation. Further, that 'truth' is absolute and determined in advance by the tester who writes the test, while the test taker needs to find out what the truth is. It does not ask the test taker to present his or her or any other possible interpretation of the truth. This is especially problematic in the testing of reading comprehension which is based on texts that are open to multiple interpretations.

Freedman (1993) notes that this phenomenon is not limited to objective items and can be extended to other test genres, such as performance-type tests. In the context of writing tests, she shows that when tests move from an indirect objective format to a direct and open type they eventually become objective. Specifically, the tests are controlled by time, content, scoring rubrics, and carefully controlled and trained raters who are led to agree on one correct answer with no deviations. This may ensure reliability but results in questionable validity as it is detached from the natural description of what writing really is. Even direct tests, then, can turn the subjective nature of the trait into an objective one: one correct answer and one truth. The 'truth', yet again, is owned by the tester who decides about the item as well as about the correct answer. This observation is important as there are those who believe that performance tests will reduce the power of tests. The case of the writing tests shows it is unlikely that performance tests will indeed change the situation, as performance tests share many features of objective items – with all the powerful uses associated with them.

Conclusions

A number of features that grant tests power have been identified in this chapter. These features enable tests to be used in powerful ways, leading to their detrimental effects and their uses by those in authority as disciplinary tools. The features described here – administration by powerful organizations, the use of the language of numbers and science, the written forms, the documentation, and the objective test formats – help to explain why tests can be used in such powerful ways.

5

Emergence of power

Emergence of tests as power tools

While tests are nowadays considered to be powerful tools used by those in authority to make and impose policy, it is interesting to note that tests, in fact, originated as tools for measuring knowledge, mostly for selection purposes. It is ironic that tests, designed in the twentieth century to provide greater opportunities and access to society's benefits, have become so powerful and authoritative. The power of tests was established in the name of equality and democracy.

The history of testing has been documented in a number of places (Ellul, 1964; Madaus, 1990; Spolsky, 1995). Throughout history, tests have been used for a variety of purposes; for example, the establishment in 210 BC of the Chinese system of civil service examinations points to the use of tests for selection, and Spolsky (1995, 1997) has demonstrated how language tests were used to enable political, social and educational control. By the middle of the nineteenth century, the value of tests for selection and control of schools started to be appreciated by the wider public; by the end of the century, in England, the use of examinations to check the progress of pupils in elementary schools, and their success in secondary schools, was firmly in place. Spolsky refers to Latham (1877) who encouraged the 'encroaching power' of examinations to take over the syllabus.

In the USA progress was equally rapid, with public acceptance of tests reaching its height in the 1920s, when tests were used by the Army to screen out unsuitable recruits. According to Madaus (1990), around the beginning of the twentieth century there was a shift in the interpretation of test scores away from a description of what a student actually knew (i.e. achievement), to a description of performance relative to a group. This shift helped to promote the construction of national norms in the 1920s for both achievement and intelligence tests. It was soon after the First World War that the movement towards standardization and conformity in education became widespread.

With the increase in population in the twentieth century and the expansion of the middle class there was a growing need for selection. Sociologists differentiate between *ascribed* and *achieved* societies. In ascribed societies the roles and functions of the citizens are predetermined, while in achieved societies individuals have rights and opportunities to find their places in the society regardless of their backgrounds and affiliations. Ascribed systems are often based on 'selection', thus operating on the assumptions that societies need to provide opportunities to those most 'deserving' them, which is often based on their backgrounds and social affiliation. Achieved systems, on the other hand, are based on democratization and operate on the assumption that everyone is given opportunities for access, especially with regard to education.

The introduction of education for all in the twentieth century was also accompanied by the introduction of tests. Both education and testing aimed to provide methods of overcoming the 'ascribed' principles and adopting the 'achieved' ones by granting opportunities to all, even to those who were not ascribed to be part of the élite and who had formerly lacked such opportunities. For example, regarding the SAT, Lemann (quoted in Schwartz, 1999: 32) noted that

> The whole point was to use the S.A.T. to X out the effect of background and create a true meritocracy. . . . The idea was that you could test the entire cohort of 17-year-olds nationally, find those with the highest scores and train them as a national leadership class.

Tests were therefore viewed as tools which could drastically overcome the ascribed principles, based on connections, class and background, and open opportunities to the wider public.

Assumptions and principles

The introduction of tests as procedures for fair selection was based on a number of principles, as listed below:

- *Tests would grant opportunities to all.* The introduction of tests would mean that every person, regardless of background, would have the opportunity and the right to be tested. If the test taker passed the test with a certain predetermined score, he or she would be selected. This was an advantage compared to the ascribed systems where only the élite had such privileges.
- *Tests would be objective.* The objectivity of tests would mean that all test takers would be treated equally with regard to name, background, gender and other factors known to contribute to subjectivity and discrimination. Information that could be viewed as subjective would not be disclosed, so the tester would not be affected by it in the decision-making process.

- *Tests would be scientific.* Tests would be viewed as scientific as they would apply a variety of methods to ensure objectivity and fairness. Concepts such as item analyses, reliability and validity based on statistical methods would guarantee both the high quality of tests and freedom from the natural biases of human beings. Such methods were to gain the trust and respect of the public, as science generally does.
- *Tests would use objective item type.* In order to minimize the biases, tests would use objective type items. Such items would neutralize the biases known to affect the judgement of testers and would reduce the subjectivity associated with the ratings and raters.

Madaus (1990) claims that the introduction of multiple choice in 1914 enabled tests to be administered *en masse*, as many more questions could be answered in the same time period, and the test could be quickly and objectively scored by unskilled clerks. The multiple-choice format was widely adopted by the test-publishing industry that emerged in the 1920s and subsequently evolved into a high enterprise. In 1926, the College Entrance Examination Board adopted the multiple-choice format for the SAT. Thus the introduction of multiple choice as an 'objective' method promoted accepted social values of technique, efficiency, standardization, conformity and accountability (Madaus, 1990).

Yet, while the above principles were meant to introduce selection tools that would turn ascribed systems into achieved ones in objective and fair ways and for all individuals, these very tools turned out to be more of an illusion than a reality. Thus, while the techniques seemed more objective, fair and scientific, they also became effective instruments for perpetuating the class differences that had existed previously.

By objectifying the tester, the items and the methods of analysis, tests turned into legitimized devices for control: unchallenged black boxes that could not be criticized, as most of those affected by tests had neither the expertise nor the knowledge to critique the tests system. Further, the 'objective' aspect of tests turned out to be an illusion, as it has since been discovered that objective tests were incapable of measuring various domains. For example, with regard to language proficiency, Spolsky (1998: 9) observed that:

> purely objective language testing appears to have failed, for while it measured something reliably, the something it measured was not the language proficiency that was assumed. The improvements that objectivity brought seem than to have been illusory.

In addition, tests have become useful instruments for central authorities to exercise power and control over individuals and educational systems. Madaus (1990) remarks that, in the 1950s, testing became the important policy technique that helped to shift educational control from local districts to the state and federal levels. A parade of federal and state legislation with standardized testing provisions contributed to a dramatic growth in the use of tests. At first test results were used to inform policy makers about the schools, but by the 1970s they had become administrative techniques to reform schools. Educational systems in different parts of the world began to recognize the authority and power of tests as efficient devices for controlling educational systems, affecting motivation, introducing curricula and defining knowledge. This was accompanied by a strong belief that it would also upgrade achievements.

The uses of tests in centralized and decentralized systems

The power of tests and their potential for control was particularly recognized and commonly used in countries with centralized educational systems (Shohamy, 1991). A centralized educational system implies that central bodies are in control of the educational system. In such systems, there was a realization that tests could be used as tools for imposing and perpetuating policies.

Shohamy (1991) observed that one test was used more often than others to affect policies and to enforce control, prestige and authority is the one administered by centralized educational systems at the end of secondary school, when students reach the age of 16 in some countries or 18 in others. That test proves to be useful for decision makers because it has a particularly strong bearing on the test takers' lives: the results of such tests determine who will graduate from secondary school and who will be allowed to continue to higher-education institutions. The end of secondary school test is therefore considered to be a high-stake test, as it affects the future of individuals by granting them permission to enter higher education and become part of that society's élite. It is, therefore, common practice in many countries, especially in those that have central educational systems, to use the end of secondary school test to establish control over major elements of the educational systems. Central agencies in a large number of systems thus use the end of high school test to control the curriculum, by using the test as a policy tool to affect the knowledge that students will be expected to acquire and the knowledge that teachers will be required to teach in schools. For example, if a central body decides that it wants its students to master a certain topic, it can make a decision to include that material as part of the end of secondary school test. In most cases this is a guarantee that students will make every effort to master the material and teachers are most likely to ensure that that material is taught in their classes, given that the test is so crucial.

It is interesting in this context to differentiate between the uses of the secondary school exit tests in centralized vs decentralized educational systems, as each is based on fundamentally different assumptions. Zack (1982) claims that in centralized systems there is a focus on the need of society to provide opportunities to those most 'deserving' of them, i.e. those who possess special talents. In decentralized systems, on the other hand, there is far less selection as there is often a belief that everyone should have the opportunity to continue into higher education. Typically, in countries where the broader social and political system is based on selection, only a small proportion of the population will enter higher education. The two systems can thus be said to function according to opposing principles, one being based on 'selection', the other on 'democratization'.

It is therefore of interest to observe how tests are used in these two opposing systems with regard to the function of the end of secondary school test. Table 5.1 displays typical features of the two systems while Table 5.2 describes the features which differentiate the uses of tests in each of the systems along a number of dimensions.

Table 5.1 Typical features of centralized vs decentralized educational systems

Decentralized	Centralized
Large proportion of students continue to higher education' all have opportunity	Small proportion of students continue to higher education
No national curriculum	National curriculum
No national ESS test	National end of school test
Formative/internal tests, by teachers	Summative predictive tests
Predictive tests (by private companies)	Summative is also predictive

Table 5.2 Uses of tests in decentralized and centralized systems (Zack, 1982)

Dimension	Decentralized	Centralized
Level of the testing body	Internal	External
Composition of the final score	Continuous	'One shot'
Content of the test	Comprehensive	High-status subjects
Proportion of students tested	High	Low
Purpose of the test	Formative/summative	Summative/predictive
Format of the test	Flexible	Uniform
Psychometric accuracy	Not known	Low to high

As can be observed in Table 5.1, in decentralized systems larger proportions of students continue to higher education while in centralized systems a substantially smaller number of students have opportunities to continue. In decentralized systems there is generally no national curriculum, no national end of secondary school test and most testing is administered in the schools by teachers and not by a centralized body; often higher education institutions will administer their own tests. In centralized systems there is often a national curriculum and a test that assesses that curriculum, leading to stricter selection whereby only a small number of students continue to higher education. The national end of secondary school test often serves both summative and predictive purposes, selecting those who are to conclude and those who are granted permission to continue their higher education.

Level of the testing body

This dimension focuses on the body that determines the items that will be included in the tests. It is a bipolar dimension that ranges from external to internal. At one end of the continuum the model posits testing bodies, testing agencies, or ministries of education that develop, administer and score the tests. At the other extreme there are internal testing bodies such as schools or even single classroom teachers who are responsible for the content, the administration and the scoring of the test. Along the continuum there are points that represent various combinations: some parts of the test may be determined by an external body; other parts may be determined internally by the teacher; and there may also be authorities who decide what the test will include and how it will be scored. The selection of the testing body can also provide a good indication of the extent to which the educational system trusts the teachers and is willing to grant them professional authority. The testing body can therefore be said to reflect the level of democratization of the educational system.

With regard to language, testing in decentralized systems is typically performed internally by classroom teachers, with no central body being responsible for the tests. In centralized systems, on the other hand, there are often high-stake tests in the main languages taught, e.g. at the end of secondary schooling. These tests are written, administered, and scored by external bodies such as national supervisors of the language who are employed by the education ministry (at times with the aid of a committee of experts) or by research institutes. It is not uncommon for a central body to have expertise in language pedagogy but no professional background or training in language testing – writing the national test is simply part of their job description. Interestingly, it is often the case that decentralized systems are committed to introducing external tests at the end of secondary school in order to gain control of the educational system. The development of the American Council on the Teaching of Foreign Languages (ACTFL, 1986) guidelines and the Oral Proficiency Interview (OPI) tests are examples of external tests aimed at providing common yardsticks to measure the learning of foreign languages by the end of secondary school in the USA (Byrnes, 1987). These procedures may be viewed as external criteria which can determine the content and scoring of language tests. Thus, the use of a test which is conducted by an external testing body provides a vehicle for controlling the content and curriculum, while the absence of centralized tests by external bodies limits the use of tests as a controlling device.

The composition of the final score

This dimension relates to the extent to which an external test score is obtained from a single, oneoff, summative instrument or from a number of formative assessments which are conducted over a period of time – be that one year or a number of years. Here, too, there are hybrids between the two poles. For example, a final score may be based simply on the results of a number of assessments which are administered throughout the school year or over a number of years. Another possibility is the administration of one external test at the end of secondary school along with a number of tests conducted throughout the school year(s); the scores obtained from both sources can be combined to render the final score. This dimension is strongly related to the selectivity criterion, with highly selective systems tending to assign great importance to a single final test. This test is often viewed as more powerful and more objective than continuous assessment, which is perceived at times as being subjective, the rationale being that a teacher who knows the student is incapable of assigning an objective judgement to that undividual. It should be noted that in some educational systems the external test score is combined with a continuous assessment which is conducted over a number of years.

The content of the test

This dimension relates to the choice of school subjects to be tested. At one end of the continuum there are the classic subjects which are perceived by the central system as being more important than others; on the other hand, there are subjects which are considered to be of less significance. The inclusion of certain subjects in an external test, say as part of the ESS test, reflects an implicit belief that these subjects are important for society and testing those subjects raises their status even further. On the other hand, the decision not to include a certain subject in a high-stake test indicates an underlying belief that the subject is not perceived as significant for the society. Often a certain subject will be included in a high-stake test but its scores will be overlooked when making decisions concerning entrance into the next level of education. In the specific case of testing foreign languages, typically, countries that view certain foreign languages as important for society will tend to include them as part of the high-stake examination. A case in point is the testing of English. In many countries English, being one of the world's most important foreign languages, is included in national examinations while other foreign languages are not. Likewise, in situations when certain subjects have low status in the society but centralized systems are interested in raising their status, they will make a decision to include them as part of the ESS test. Centralized systems tend to test mostly high prestige and high status subjects which grants them more power and status.

Proportion of students tested

This dimension relates to the extent to which tests, especially ESS tests, are used for selection. In countries where compulsory education has been extended to the age of 16 and higher, all students are entitled to graduate from secondary school and there is a need for a selection device to determine those who will be entitled to continue to post-secondary education. On the other hand, however, in countries where only a proportion of the population is entitled to enter secondary school, the ESS test serves as a device to decide those who will be allowed to continue their studies. In these situations, the 'threat' of a test as a selection device is often encountered well before the examination is actually taken. A school may in fact accept or reject students based on the assessment of the likelihood that the student will be able to pass the high-stake test. In this dimension there is a differentiation among how systems use high-stake tests, such as the ESS, as a selection criterion for higher education. At one end of the selection spectrum there are systems which use tests for selection while, at the other, there are systems that rely only slightly on the ESS test as a criterion for selection. Countries with strong democratization principles allow relatively large numbers of students to graduate from secondary school, and often will not use any form of secondary school external test.

In a number of European countries tests are administered both at ages 16 and 18. Those with poor results (in some countries as many as 80 per cent) are forced to leave school or to engage in vocational programmes. Those who are allowed to continue in schools are often required to take yet another examination at the end of secondary school.

A typical situation in the case of language testing is one in which obtaining a high grade in the ESS examination in English as a Foreign Language is among the most important criteria for graduation from secondary school and acceptance to post-secondary studies. In some situations it serves as the single criterion. By contrast, in countries which are based on democratization, a student's score in English or in any other foreign language does not affect their opportunity to be accepted to post-secondary education.

Purpose of the test

This dimension relates to the specific purpose of the test – whether it is *formative*, *summative* or *predictive*. Formative testing refers to assessment on an ongoing basis, as part of the learning process in the classroom. Summative testing is aimed at examining the extent to which the student has acquired the material covered in the curriculum. Predictive testing provides information about the probable future performance of the test taker, in college or in other contexts.

The terms *achievement* and *proficiency* describe further distinctions that can be made in the overall purpose of testing in the specific context of language testing. Achievement refers to the mastery of the language learned in a specific course of study, while proficiency seeks to measure the language competence that the student will bring to real life in a specific, future, well-defined context.

In terms of the uses of tests in this dimension, high-stake exams such as those administered at the end of secondary school are often used both for summative and predictive purposes and as indicators of both achievement and proficiency. On the other hand, in a decentralized system, the ESS test is used mostly for formative and summative purposes, as a part of measuring achievement integrated into the learning and teaching process. Thus, the adoption of the ACTFL proficiency guidelines and the Oral Proficiency Interview in the USA indicates a shift from testing for formative purposes to testing for summative and predictive purposes, and from achievement to proficiency.

Format of the test

This dimension refers to whether the format of the test is uniform or flexible. At one end of the continuum the assessment is uniform, which means that similar test formats are given to all test takers; at the other end, assessment is flexible, implying that there are alternative formats of assessment such as projects, self-assessment, informal assessment, and other procedures which require application of knowledge, whether internally or externally. Flexible assessment means, therefore, that the score which the test taker obtains is based on a variety of different types of performance and not just on a single test. It is often the case that in centralized systems the assessment is uniform; it is a test which is administered by an external body. In systems which are decentralized it is often the case that a number of options are available, especially in situations when internal assessment is practised.

Psychometric accuracy

This dimension relates to the extent to which a high-stake test meets psychometric criteria of reliability and validity. At one end of the continuum there are tests for which there is no evidence of psychometric accuracy, although the tests may be administered to a large number of people and can be considered as 'high stake'. At the other end, there is no information as to the psychometric traits of the test and no follow-ups in terms of the use of the tests and their effect on test takers, teaching and learning. Centralization, then, does not necessarily guarantee high-quality tests. Information regarding the psychometric accuracy of tests in decentralized systems, especially tests used in the classroom, is not available, but there is a general belief that psychometric accuracy is not considered to be a major concern of classroom teachers.

Uses of tests as a means for control

Typical are situations when tests are introduced in order to select those who are most suited for continuation to higher education. While in the past this type of selection would have been performed through personal connection, financial status, etc., the introduction of tests meant that the criteria for selecting the best students was more objective, as each student had the chance of being selected to continue to higher education. Yet, the fact that the test had such a detrimental impact on students' lives – i.e. controlling the opportunity to enter higher education, which in most countries is the key to success or failure in society and life in general – meant that tests became extremely powerful tools. It was in the hands of testers to determine success or failure. The recognition of the power of tests, means that tests are used as disciplinary tools to perpetuate, impose and control specific behaviours and agendas. In this example, this means that since decision makers, in this case educational bureaucrats, realize that the results of the test have such an influence on students' lives, they use the power of tests to make students study to attain that knowledge which they perceive as important. It is clear to them that students will do anything to maximize their opportunity to succeed on those high-stake tests in order to be selected. The test then became the tool through which knowledge, as perceived by testers, was defined. In this example then, the test changed its role from a device used to measure knowledge to a method through which knowledge is imposed and perpetuated. For both the tester and the test taker the test is a means to an end. For the test taker the test is secondary, it is merely a method of obtaining an opportunity; for the educationalist the test is a method of imposing the acquisition of certain knowledge. The extent to which the students master the topic is secondary, the primary goal is to make teachers teach and students study specific topics, as it is clear that the act of testing *per se* will perpetuate such behaviour. Tests then become the tools that have the power to affect knowledge.

These situations occur repeatedly in the classroom where teachers decide to introduce tests when they feel that students have not mastered certain material. The introduction of the test, by itself, is likely to make students change their behaviour – that is, to study at home or at class.

A similar phenomenon may occur when a principal who is not happy with the achievement of the students imposes a test in the school at the end of the year or when a nation decides to introduce national tests in order to upgrade the national achievement of a country. In fact, this use of tests to change behaviour occurs at all levels – teachers with students, principals with teachers, regional officials with principals and national authorities with regional officials. Or it may be a reason why countries join international competitions, such as the International Evaluation Association (IEA). In all these cases those who introduce the tests are not interested in the results of the tests *per se*, but rather in causing a change of behaviour in learning and teaching. If the test had no power it would not have been introduced in the first place. Thus the test becomes a method of introducing a behavioural change. The power of the test, as expressed in the fear and respect that those affected by the test have for it, guarantees an almost automatic response – behaviours will be changed.

Clearly, this process has a stronger impact when the tests are potentially detrimental to the test takers – a situation termed 'high stake' against 'low stake' where the test has little detrimental effect on test takers. It should also be noted that whether the test is in fact detrimental is not the issue. At times this may be real; at others it is only the perception of the test takers that matters. Yet, tests are viewed as detrimental regardless of their actual or intended use. As will be shown later, at times the intention of those who introduced the tests was in fact not to use them as detrimental tools; yet this intention cannot be fully controlled as there may be other bodies which will use the tests for such a purpose.

The recognition of the strong power of tests was especially noticed by decision makers in education, politics and commerce, who started using tests as disciplinary tools for affecting the behaviour of those whose future is dependent on the results of tests. At present, therefore, tests are used more as authoritative and disciplinary tools for exercising power and control than for objective and democratic purposes of selection.

Conclusions

The introduction of tests for making decisions regarding selection provided an opportunity for a shift from 'ascribed' societies, which granted entrance based on biased criteria, to 'achieved' societies where all have an equal chance of being selected. Yet, in spite of the opportunity for all to be tested, the use of scientific and objective methods and item-type tests served as a method of perpetuating existing differences, as those who wrote the tests used their own knowledge as criteria for entrance.

At the same time, in many societies, in particular in centralized systems, the primary role of tests – especially of high-stake tests such as those administered at the end of secondary school – changed from measuring knowledge to enabling centralized bodies to control education, content, learning and teaching. High-stake tests are used by central bodies as a method of controlling and dictating much of what happens in the educational system and in society as a whole. Yet, the use of tests varies by the type of educational system – centralized or decentralized. Each of the systems uses the following devices to control the system: the testing body, the composition of the final score, the content of the test, the proportion of students tested, and the purpose, format and psychometric accuracy of the test.

6

Temptations

In addition to the built-in features that allow their powerful uses, tests possess certain characteristics that provide decision makers with attractive benefits that tempt them to use tests for policy making. This chapter will discuss these characteristics in order to better understand the advantages that decision makers obtain from tests.

Tests are perceived by the public as authoritative

Using tests for policy making has strong authoritative power, as in most cases those who are affected by tests tend to change their behaviours in line with the demands of the test. Once a test becomes a method of control, supported by central bodies, it rarely faces any objection by those who are subjects of the test; results obtained from tests are generally viewed as final and absolute and are therefore rarely challenged. The main reason, as explained in Chapters 3 and 4, is that tests are administered on behalf of powerful organizations, while test takers are independent individuals who are often powerless.

Tests allow flexible cutting scores

A major temptation for policy makers to use tests, is that tests allow users to determine cutting scores in arbitrary ways and thus create quotas in a flexible manner. Cutting scores are specific points that serve as the basis for decisions on quotas etc., such as the number of people who will pass a given test, enter special programmes, obtain certificates or be granted entrance visas. A low cutting score means that many people will pass the test; a high one means that fewer people will pass, entitling those who do pass to the privileges associated with the test. Though, over the years, a number of methods have been developed to determine cutting scores accurately, the issue is still very controversial and remains unresolved.

Cutting scores are often used by those in authority as 'gate-keeping' tools – barriers to those who are not wanted. A demonstration of how cutting scores are used in flexible ways for political manipulation is given in Chapter 11, with regard to a teacher education test in the state of Massachusetts, USA. In that case the Board of Education raised the passing grade for teachers' certification examinations; as a result almost 60 per cent of the prospective teachers who took the test failed. In another example, cutting scores were used to determine the number of immigrants allowed to enter a certain country. In yet another example (presented in Chapter 8), cutting scores were used in one year to prove that an unusually high number of students had difficulties in reading comprehension, while in another year the decision regarding cutting scores led to a completely different conclusion. Thus, cutting scores provide a major temptation to decision makers when they are using tests for policy making.

Tests are effective for control and for redefining knowledge

An additional temptation for decision makers to use tests is that they allow those in authority to control and manipulate knowledge. Specifically, by including certain contents and topics on tests the tester can redefine and introduce specific knowledge according to his or her perceptions or perspective. This is inevitable, since test takers tend to adopt and internalize their knowledge according to the requirements of the test. As was noted in Chapter 3, test takers will do this to maximize their scores, given the detrimental effects of the tests. In the three studies described in Chapters 8, 9 and 10, the content of the tests became the *de facto* curriculum and was significantly more important than the existing curriculum. Pedagogical bodies have generally very little supervision of the content of tests. Shepard (1991) shows how the decision of what is included in a test is the prerogative of the testing experts and is often in contradiction to the knowledge base as defined by the subject experts. Thus, it is very tempting for those who introduce tests to use them as a means for creating, redefining and controlling knowledge.

Freedman (1993) notes that exams are popular among policy makers because they provide one of the few levers on the curriculum that policy makers can control. Not having tests means that teachers are free to create their own curriculum, their own means and content of instruction. It is therefore of no surprise that in situations when the status of teachers is low, decision makers choose to use tests to control classroom teaching and dictate what will be taught by teachers and learned by students, both in and out of the classroom.

Controlling knowledge through tests is also typical in the political and policy contexts. In two cases described in Chapter 11 – Latvia and Australia – tests were used to dictate and control the languages that the candidates were expected to master. In the example of the teacher education test in Massachusetts, the test defined and controlled the knowledge that prospective teachers were expected to have.

Tests have strong appeal to the public, especially parents

The introduction of tests has a strong appeal to the public as it symbolizes social order in areas in which the public normally feels a lack of control, such as education. Using tests is interpreted by the public as a sign of a serious and meaningful attitude towards education and as evidence of action on the part of government.

House (1998) notes that in the USA tests have been repeatedly embraced by both political parties. Politics, he claims, seems to drive these reforms, and when objections are raised by testing experts that critical technical tasks cannot be accomplished, the experts are overriden. He also claims that the so far successful attempts by the Republican party in the USA to object to the proposal of President Clinton for national tests, is one of the few cases where such a protest has been successful. Yet this can be explained by a number of political and unrelated factors, by objections to President Clinton's educational and other policies and not necessarily by objections to tests.

As was noted by Bourdieu (1991), and as discussed at length in Chapter 15, tests often serve the needs of certain groups in society to perpetuate their power and dominance and are, thus, rarely challenged. Tests have the wide support of parents, as they are perceived as educational and symbolize social order. For parents who often do not trust schools and teachers, tests provide reassuring signs of control and order. Tests are familiar for most parents who were exposed to tests in their own formative years. Tests symbolize control and discipline and are perceived as an indication of effective learning. It is often observed that raising the educational standards through testing appeals to the middle classes, partly because it means gaining access to better jobs for their children and also because, for some, it is a code word for restricting minority access (House, 1998). The paradox is that low-status parents, minorities and immigrants who are constantly excluded by tests, have an overwhelming respect for them and often fight against their abandonment.

Tests are useful for delivering 'objective proofs'

Owing to the authority and trust that tests have in the eyes of the public, evidence obtained from them serves as proof for a whole range of arguments. The types of interaction taking place between the testers and test takers are based on the assumption that the tester has a neutral, non-participatory role in the testing process, while the test results provide the evidence and proof. Reference is often made to 'The *test* demonstrated that you are a failure' or 'The *test* showed that you did not study hard enough'. Such statements put the burden of proof on the results of the test, while the tester remains a neutral observer, shrugging off all types of responsibilities.

Foucault (1979) notes that it is only in this century that the tester made the test an 'objective unobtrusive' messenger. In the past the tester had to face the test taker directly and share the responsibility for the testing verdict. Similarly, MacIntyre (1984) notes that bureaucrats tend to adjust means to ends and deploy scientific knowledge organized in terms of universal quasi-legal generalizations to help them to prove claims.

Using tests as proof also occurs in the classroom, where it is not un-common for teachers to give tests when students are misbehaving; the 'low' score obtained on such tests is then used as proof of 'bad behaviour' that leads to low achievement. Flexible cutting scores serve as useful gimmicks that testers often use when they employ tests as tools for proof.

In one of the cases reported in Chapter 11, an entrance examination included grammar rather than communicative knowledge, in order to prove to the students – who had studied a foreign language for several years – that they were actually incompetent in the language and should therefore re-enrol in a beginners' language class.

Tests allow cost-effective and efficient policy making

Using tests as disciplinary tools is a cost-effective strategy for policy making. In comparison to introducing reforms through teacher training, development of new curricula or new textbooks, changing the tests is a substantially cheaper venture. House (1998) notes, for example, that it was difficult to see how new national educational initiatives could emerge under the Clinton government when the Department of Education had neither the money nor the agency capabilities to provide leadership. It was at that point that the primary reform strategy relied on introducing the standards-and-testing initiative. Thus, it became the centrepiece of the Clinton administration.

Obtaining funds is often a long process that is not possible to complete in the short time that bureaucrats hold office. Tests, therefore, provide policy makers with the opportunity to create policy in the shortest time. In the situation of the English oral tests, reported in Chapter 10, the Ministry of Education announced the content of the new final examination one year before the test was to be administered. This guaranteed that the new content was included in the school and class curriculum within ten months – the time between the announcement of the change and the actual administration of the test.

Tests provide those in authority with visibility and evidence of action

A different temptation for policy makers in using tests is the perception of bureaucrats, as well as of the public at large, that introducing tests provides evidence of action. For bureaucrats this offers a major advantage over other ways of making policy. The example of the Arabic test discussed in Chapter 11 is a case in point; although the national supervisor of Arabic was aware that the introduction of the test did not fulfil any of his expectations and intentions regarding raising the achievement and the status of the subject, he was still determined to keep the test. The introduction of the test provided him with visibility and evidence of action. Similar patterns can be observed in classrooms where some teachers overuse testing as a 'teaching' strategy.

Conclusions

Tests offer decision makers attractive temptations. They are capable of perpetuating authority and reinforcing control. Tests have great appeal to the public, especially parents, who perceive tests as a sign of discipline and of quality education. Furthermore, tests offer decision makers the temptation to redefine knowledge according to set agendas, especially by using flexible cutting scores. In addition, tests provide decision makers with a cost-effective and efficient device for making policy. From a political view, the use of tests grants policy makers evidence of action and visibility. With such a long list of attractive benefits it is clear why decision makers are so tempted to use tests so frequently. This temptation is further reinforced as the public generally does not prevent or protest such uses, as tests are considered to be a domain that only professionals in the field are allowed to enter and to express their views. The result is that tests are used in unmonitored ways, with no examination of their consequences.

Part

II

Uses of tests: studies and cases

7

Domains of inquiry

Two domains were selected as the foci of the studies on the use of tests – *intentions* and *effects*. Intentions refers to the rationale, purposes and expectations of decision makers in introducing and using tests; effects refers to the *post-priori* use of tests, focusing on the impact and consequences of tests with regard to education and other areas on which tests may impact. An important aspect of these two domains is the connection between them, i.e. whether the intentions in using tests actually materialize and whether tests lead to effects and consequences regardless of specific intentions.

Intentions

Intentions address the purposes, objectives and expectations of decision makers upon deciding to introduce tests, especially those tests that are referred to as 'high stake' as these tend to have detrimental effects for individuals.

There are very few studies that have systematically examined the rationale, intentions and expectations for introducing tests. Data about intentions are not easily obtained, as intentions are seldom fully discussed publicly. There is, therefore, a distinction between *overt* and *covert* intentions. Overt intentions refer to agendas that are open to the public generally, through the publication of formal documents disseminated by the bodies that introduced the tests. These can be teachers (introducing classroom tests), principals (introducing school-wide tests), officials in the Ministry of Education (introducing state-wide large-scale tests) or other agencies such as ministries of immigration, economics, labour or commerce. Covert intentions refer to agendas that are not known to the public and can only be inferred and deduced from other sources. One reason that intentions are not stated explicitly is that they may be interpreted by some as indications of discrimination or indirect intervention in areas which are not under the authority of those introducing the tests.

Another distinction with regard to intentions is between *intended* and *unintended*. While the body introducing the tests may have specific intentions (whether overt or covert), unintended outcomes may emerge as a result of the test, even though these outcomes were not meant to happen. These are situations when decision makers did not plan for the outcomes but they happened anyway, often in spite of the intentions.

Effects

While there is very little knowledge about intentions behind the introduction of tests, there is a fast growing body of knowledge and a large number of studies that have examined effects. A distinction is often made between *educational* and *societal* effects. The first refers to the changes as a result of tests in areas such as curriculum, teaching methods, learning strategies, materials, assessment practices and knowledge tested, while societal effects are concerned with the effects of tests on aspects such as gate-keeping, ideology, ethicality, morality and fairness.

Messick (1981, 1989, 1996) was the first to draw attention to the topic of impact, claiming that the consequences of tests should be incorporated into a broader perspective of a unified concept of validity. He argued that because the social values played a part in the intended and unintended outcomes of test interpretation and use which derive from the meaning of the test scores, appraisal of the social consequences of the testing should be subsumed as an aspect of construct validity (1996: 251).

There are a number of issues of concern with regard to the effects of tests. One relates to the terminology while the other refers to research that examines the types of effect and the factors that affect it.

Terminology

At least four terms refer to the effect of tests: *washback*, *impact*, *consequences* and *effect*. All of these terms are used to refer to phenomena associated with changes in behaviour as a result of a test, and they are often used interchangeably. Effect is used to encompass washback, impact and consequences. Distinction between washback and impact is made by Hamp-Lyons (1997) who claims that washback refers to the effect and influence that the introduction of tests has on the educational context, while impact is a broader term referring to effects on education and society. Alderson and Wall (1993) define washback (or 'backwash') as the phenomenon where, because of the test, teachers and learners do things they would not normally do, hence encompassing the notion of influence.

Messick (1996: 251) further claims that 'in the context of unified validity, evidence of washback is an instance of the consequential aspect of construct validity'. Thus, Messick's concept of unified validity seems to be the bridge between the narrow range of effects included in washback, and the broader one encompassed by 'impact' which includes '. . . evidence and rationales for evaluating the intended and unintended consequences of tests . . . interpretation and use . . . unfairness in test use, and positive or negative washback effects on teaching and learning'.

The term 'consequences' is generally used by Messick to encompass all three but with a stronger focus on ideological values. This is also how the term is used in Chapter 8 to discuss the societal influences of tests. Messick notes that washback is the only form of testing consequence that needs to be weighed when evaluating validity, and testing consequences is only one aspect of construct validity leading to the term *consequential validity*. This includes evidence and rationales for evaluating the intended and unintended consequences of score interpretation and use in both the short and the long term '. . . [and] unfairness in test use, and positive or negative washback effects on teaching and learning' (Messick, 1996: 251). An additional term often used to refer to the connection between learning and instruction is 'systemic validity' (Fredriksen and Collins, 1989) relating to the introduction of tests into the educational system, along with additional variables which are part of the learning and instructional system. In such a situation a test becomes part of a dynamic process in which changes in the educational system take place according to feedback obtained from the test. Similar terms associated with the impact of tests on learning are *measurement driven instruction*, referring to the notion that tests drive learning, and *curriculum alignment*, implying that the curriculum is modified according to test results.

Types of impact

With regard to types of impact there is a focus on *who* is responsible for test impact and *what* the nature of the impact is. Some view the responsibility for introducing impact to lie beyond the test developers. Hamp-Lyons (1997: 298) argues that it is not only the test developers whose work has impact, but also testing agencies who make policy and economic decisions about the kinds of testing to support. Textbook publishers make the economic decisions about the kinds of textbooks that teachers and parents will buy to 'ensure' that their children are ready for the test, as well as school districts and boards, ministries of education, and national or federal governments, who bow to pressure to account for the progress of pupils and the value-added effect of education. (These questions are also dealt with in Chapter 18 in the discussion of 'Who is the tester?'.)

Most of the research on impact has focused on one type, that of washback, while substantially less work is available on the impact of tests on society.

Alderson and Wall (1993: 115–29) present a number of washback hypotheses which they claim need to be researched. A test can influence teaching and learning: what teachers teach, how teachers teach, what learners learn, how learners learn, the rate and sequence of learning, and attitude to the content and methods of teaching and learning. They further attempt to explore the concept by asking: 'How directly, according to the washback hypothesis, do tests bring about change in teaching and learning?' (1993: 18). A simplistic view, they claim, would assume that the fact of a test having a set of qualities is sufficient in itself, by virtue of the importance of tests in most societies in bringing about change. However, this assumption takes little account of other educational factors which influence teaching, such as teachers' competence and their understanding of the principles underlying the test, and levels of resources within the school system. They propose refinement to the basic washback hypothesis by distinguishing the content of teaching from methodology used, and teaching from learning. They further emphasize the need to consider the impact of a test not only on teaching and learning but also on attitudes, materials and effort, and that in order to understand washback there is a need to consider factors such as personality, the consequences of performance in the test and the learners' perceptions of those consequences.

Issues regarding the nature of washback focus mostly on whether washback is good or bad, positive or negative. Alderson and Wall argue that if it is a 'good' test (i.e. reflecting the aims of the syllabus and its content and method) then it will produce positive washback; if it is a 'bad' test then it will produce negative washback. However, others (e.g. Ferman, 1998) have argued that washback hypotheses may also imply that a 'poor' test could conceivably have a 'good' impact if it made the learners and teachers do 'good' things, such as increase learning activities. Likewise, a good test may have negative consequences; indeed, good or bad it will have beneficial washback if it increases learning activities and intentions, making teachers and learners work harder. Still others claim there is no such thing as a good test, as the harm of examinations lie in the restrictions they impose on curricula, teachers and students and in their encouragement of mechanical, boring and debilitating forms of teaching and learning (Oxenham, 1984).

Spolsky (1995: 56) argues that the inevitable outcome of examinations is, repeatedly, narrowing the educational process.

> Once the content of an examination has been bruited it becomes more or less the precise specification of what knowledge or behavior will be rewarded (or will avoid punishment). No reasonable teacher will do other than focus his or her pupils' efforts on the specific items that are to be tested; no bright pupil will want to spend the time on anything but preparation for what is to be on the examination. The control of the instructional process then is transferred from those most immediately concerned (the teacher and the pupil) to the examination itself.

Research on impact

Research on effects, impact and consequences of language tests has emerged mostly in the past decade and its main focus has been on case studies where new tests were introduced (Shepard, 1991; Smith, 1991). Research on impact is known to be difficult as there is often no base line to compare, it takes a long time to observe, and is seldom visible to the researcher as it can occur outside the domains which the researcher examines.

The main findings point to the complex reality of impact, especially in the case of high-stake tests. A study by Alderson and Hamp-Lyons (1996) discovered that the influence of the test on what happens in TOEFL preparation classes, compared with non-TOEFL preparation classes by the same teacher, was in fact more complex than the theory of washback would anticipate. Watanabe (1996) reports a similarly complex picture emerging from a study of the impact of university entrance tests in EFL in Japan. Wall (1996) and Wall and Alderson (1998) analysed the wide range of factors modulating the washback of a progressive test reform in a traditional educational system in Sri Lanka. Similarly, Cheng (1998) examined the effect of a new English test in Hong Kong and found that the introduction of the test successfully changed the 'what' in teaching but the extent to which it changed the 'how' was limited, so the changes were superficial. In terms of impact of language tests on content areas, Peirce and Stein (1995) showed how tests affect the interpretation of reading passages, as the social occasion and the power relations between students and tester changed. Specifically, it was demonstrated that students who were in a powerless position in testing situations could not refuse to take the test and were forced to look for the exact answers the test makers intended, which were often different from their own.

In terms of the impact of tests on minority student immigrants and both genders in school settings, concern centres on how test items work differently for specific groups. A number of techniques, such as Differential Item Functioning (DIF), were developed to identify biased items. Yet, some of these methods have been criticized as insufficient; Elder (1997), for example, showed how the technique involves questions of values in the choice of the criterion adopted as the benchmark in the comparison of groups. Thus, the bias depends on a definition of the test construct, which is often defined in political terms.

The three studies presented in Chapters 8–10 (see also Shohamy, 1993, 1994, 1997, 1998) and the cases in Chapter 11 provide empirical data and observations regarding the uses of tests by focusing on intentions involved in using the tests and their effects and consequences. In other words, given the power of tests and their detrimental forces, what are the intentions of those in authority when they introduce tests, what are the tests used for and what are their effects on education and society?

8

A reading comprehension test

The context

In a large number of countries, especially those that have centralized educational systems (see Chapter 5 for distinction on the use of tests in centralized vs decentralized education systems), tests are used for purposes of monitoring and controlling the education systems. Tests such as the NAEP (National Achievement of Educational Performance) are used as tools to assess 'the state of the nation' in certain educational domains. It should be noted that in addition to national tests of this type there are international achievement tests whereby the participating nations not only examine their own performances but are also eager to compare their achievements with those of other countries. While such national or international tests are very common in most of the developed countries of the world (the IEA organization represents about 50 countries), there are very few studies that examine the rationale for using these tests, i.e. why countries choose to administer such tests. Thus, questions need to be asked as to the reasons for introducing tests, the use of the results and the effects of the results on education and society. The reading comprehension test, discussed in this chapter, is typical of other types of test which are regularly administered in many countries for monitoring achievement. This type of test is especially used in countries with centralized education systems that have both a national curriculum and national examinations. The study that is presented here specifically examines aspects of the use of this type of test (Shohamy, 1993, 1994, 1997, 1998). It is a national test, the aim of which is to assess and monitor the level of national achievement in reading comprehension. The study closely observed the intentions of using the test and its short- and long-range effects. As will be demonstrated here, the act of administering this large-scale test had far-reaching effects, well beyond the intentions expected and declared by those who introduced it.

Background

In 1993 the Ministry of Education in a certain country decided to administer a national test for measuring the reading comprehension levels of all fourth and fifth grade students. The test was administered to 160,000 students, in 6000 classes, in 1600 schools employing 6000 external proctors. In terms of its content, the format of the test was made up of short passages followed by questions pertaining to the text and the vocabulary included in it. The test included 60 questions: 15 were defined as representing the minimal level of reading (answering two of the questions incorrectly resulted in a failed score) while the remainder were norm-referenced, in which the score was reported as the number of correct answers.

The administration of the test was accompanied by extensive media attention, as well as strong resentment on the part of the teachers. The results were disseminated in a special news conference at which it was reported that 33 per cent of students had failed the test. A map of the country was shown on national television, highlighting cities and areas in which a large number of students had failed. It was a major news event, with almost 500 newspaper articles published about the topic, mostly focusing on the implications of the results with regard to political, social, economic and educational dimensions. Owing to massive public criticism, the test was cancelled after two years of administration. In 1998, a new reading comprehension test was developed, to be administered by a professional testing institute.

Intentions

Prior to the administration of the test, the intentions and rationale for introducing the reading comprehension test were stated in a letter that was disseminated by the Ministry of Education to the parents of children who were taking the test. The letter is presented below:

Dear Parent
    The Ministry of Education and Culture is about to administer tests in math and reading comprehension to all the students. The results of the tests will enable us to find out about the level of achievement of children in this important subject. It will help the schools plan their work for the following year. The results will be used by the Ministry for pedagogical purposes only, for follow up, for research and for establishing policy. The data will be confidential and kept in the data base of the Ministry of Education in accordance with the Privacy Law (1981). The detailed results will be sent to the school after the beginning of the next academic year.

The letter portrays the test as educational, helpful, constructive and pedagogical. Moreover, there is concern as to the potential misuse of the results, so confidentiality is ensured. Yet, as will be shown in this chapter, even with the best of intentions, it is difficult to predict the effects and consequences of tests, especially high-stake tests, as they tend to have a stronger impact on the behaviours of those who are affected by test results. As will be shown, tests are not neutral as they impact on a large number of dimensions.

Effects on education

The effects of the reading comprehension test on the educational system were examined through interviews with teachers and analysis of teaching material that was produced after the results had been disseminated.

Teaching materials and workshops

The test stimulated teachers and regional supervisors to produce ample new material for teaching reading comprehension. The material included worksheets and textbooks. About 30 books and workbooks were published; supervisors developed practice pages and worksheets identical to those used on the test. Most of these were clones of the test – that is, they included reading comprehension texts that were often followed by multiple-choice questions, which was very different from the official curriculum. Workshops for teaching reading comprehension were offered around the country, and teachers were asked to attend them.

Teaching and allocation of classroom time

The test affected the allocation of time, with a large number of teaching sessions being diverted into reading comprehension sessions; thus the number of hours allocated to the subject increased substantially. This is important because previously no special hours had been allocated to the teaching of reading comprehension; rather, it had been integrated into all school subjects. Now, however, content areas such as geography, history, etc. were turned into reading comprehension sessions. Yet, reading comprehension was taught entirely in terms of 'test activities'. Teachers who previously had a broad view of literacy, turned exclusively to the teaching of reading comprehension in identical ways to those used in the test. At the same time, teachers claimed that they were at a loss regarding the specific teaching methods and strategies they should adopt in order to teach it.

Interpretation of test scores

Since no guidance was provided regarding the meaning and interpretation of the test scores, there was an extensive misuse of the results. Teachers were blamed for the students' failure by both principals and parents. This was the case with one teacher who, because she felt it suited her students, was using a teaching method different from those that her principal had recommended. She claimed that the failure of her class had nothing to do with her teaching method, but that they had failed because her class contained five new immigrants and five disabled children. Nevertheless, the principal used the results to convict her of having used the wrong teaching method, and the teacher was not allowed to teach that class the following year. On the other hand, teachers whose class did well on the test were rewarded and praised.

Teachers' attitudes

By and large, while principals and other administrators thought it was a good idea to introduce the test, teachers felt that it was unnecessary. Some teachers thought that the test was humiliating and unfair, and that the results simply confirmed what they already knew about their students. On the basis of interviews with ten teachers – five of whom had classes that failed – the most obvious impact found was 'emotional'. Teachers whose classes failed spoke with great passion about the test; they expressed anger and frustration, and were very critical of it. They claimed that they had been wrongly blamed for the failure of their classes as the fault lay with the student population. The teachers complained that the test did not reflect the material they had taught and that the format of the test did not reflect their way of teaching reading comprehension. Furthermore, they reported that they had not been told in advance what would be tested and that the unfamiliar format must have increased students' anxiety and affected their performance. They also said that they felt humiliated by the test, specifically because they had not been consulted about it and it therefore did not reflect their teaching. They claimed that in many cases they were blamed by the principals for the poor performance of their students and in general perceived the test as an intrusion of an external body in their teaching. They also felt that they should have had a choice concerning who was to be tested, to enable them to protect their students.

Effect on society and individuals

Beyond the effects of the test on educational dimensions the study also examined the effect of the test on individuals and society using a perspective suggested by Foucault in *Discipline and Punish*, whereby tests are viewed as disciplinary tools. According to Foucault (1979: 184), an examination can be interpreted as an act of power and control (see also Chapter 3):

> The examination combines the technique of an observing hierarchy and those of normalizing judgment. It is a normalizing gaze, a *surveillance* that makes it possible to *quantify*, *classify* and *punish*. It establishes over individuals a visibility through which one differentiates and *judges* them.

> (Author's italics)

By using the descriptors suggested by Foucault, it can be shown that the reading comprehension test, in fact, exemplifies disciplinary features of surveillance, quantification, classification, judgement, sanctions, scaling and standardizing of population, frightening, deterring, and demonstrating authority. The evidence for these claims is presented below.

An act of surveillance

Using Foucault's descriptors, the test was admittedly an act of surveillance by the educational system, as the educational system could follow the progress of all the children in the country. Without asking permission from parents, students or teachers, the ministry can compel children to be tested. It can enter the classroom and demand that all the children in the country take a test to show what they know in reading comprehension according to the educational system's criteria. If in fact the system did not intend to use the results of the test for the selection of individuals, why were students asked to write their name? Why were their scores released to schools by students' names? In administering the tests, the education system did not have to prove that the tests were not 'harmful' to the students or that the tests were of such high quality that they provide accurate scores. Students or parents have no rights, nor do they have the tools to examine the quality of the test beforehand. All students are obliged to participate, and if they refuse they or their teachers may be punished. The performance of each of these students is then recorded in the form of a number which is classified as pass or fail. The education system now has records on each of its pupils in reading comprehension.

The information that the education system can obtain from this surveillance cannot be of a very high quality, since the decision on who failed and who passed was based on a limited number of questions. The results do not take into consideration the relevance of the texts to the background of the students, their social and ethnic environment, their home culture – especially the environment of the immigrant population – nor whether the students had a good or bad day when doing the test. But it is not only students who are surveyed; so are teachers and schools. The documented, recorded and classified information also related to teachers, suggesting that whether the students succeeded or failed the reading comprehension depended on the teacher's abilities.

An act of quantification

Once the scores were disseminated, students and teachers were then on the records of the database of the education system according to their scores in reading comprehension. The education system now has records on each of its pupils in reading comprehension. Thus, their identity is now described, defined and summarized in terms of 'percent of correct answers', in this case, on a limited number of test questions and texts.

An act of classification

In addition to the ability to test anyone, at anytime, and to quantify students, another aspect of power and control is classification of all students as successes or failures, good or bad, based on their scores on the reading comprehension test. It was then possible for the Ministry of Education to classify and rank students, teachers and schools into categories. Often the students, schools and teachers are not even aware that they have been classified as successes or failures.

Scaling and standardizing populations

The reading comprehension test was used for standardization and controlling the learning, as teachers and students began to follow identical formats for teaching reading comprehension – short texts followed by questions – in preparation for the administration of the test the following year. This test-like teaching became the new *de facto* curriculum, overriding the existing curriculum. While each of the students was an individual case before the test, after the tests he or she was judged in relation to all the other students of similar age in the country. It is important to mention that the norm for a country is determined, in most cases, by how the remainder of the country performs on the same reading comprehension questions, as the same test is given throughout the country. Thus, the test has the power to standardize the deviation in the country. Whereas this year there may have been some deviations as a result of the different backgrounds, different teachers, different learning contexts and different ways of constructing meaning, the effect of this test will be to ensure that this will not happen again and that students around the country will construct meaning in the same way, ending up with exactly the same knowledge.

Foucault includes the description given in Figure 8.1 to visualize the notion of standardization. This is a description of the process by which tests standardize the population to own identical knowledge.

Figure 8.1 N. Andry, *L'orthopédie ou l'art de prévenir et de corriger dans les enfants les difformités du corps* (Orthopaedics or the art of preventing and correcting deformities of the body in children). 1749.

An act of judgement and sanctions

Once the information is available (observed, documented, quantified and classified) there is legitimacy for imposing sanctions. Examples of sanctions were forbidding students from entering a certain class level, and demanding that they repeat grades and withdraw from upgrading programmes. In some schools teachers were dismissed, textbooks were changed and students were placed in low level groups based on tests that were initially intended only to evaluate the level of schools.

An act of demonstrating authority

Tests are often used for the purpose of declaring where authority lies; this is especially true in centralized systems. In many developed countries responsibility and authority are shared by one body. In some countries there is a clear distinction between authority and responsibility. The introduction of the test provided the Ministry of Education with a proof of action that has high visibility.

It is often the case that tests are conducted by ministries of education when they feel that their authority has been threatened, or when they feel that they are losing control; the use of the test helps to bring power back to the authority. The administration of national tests of any kind is often aimed at indicating who is in charge. This is especially true when the system fails on other fronts. The reading comprehension test was administered by the Ministry of Education, to a large extent as a reaction to complaints that innovations and new programmes in reading comprehension were not being introduced into the system. Similarly, the introduction of the ACTFL guidelines in the USA was a reaction to criticism that there were no new programmes in foreign language teaching and that children were not performing as expected. Though no new programmes have been introduced recently, the administration of the test is an indication to the public that something is being done.

The tensions between the authority and those who are responsible for introducing the change are clear in the case of the reading comprehension test. One wonders whether teachers, those responsible for implementing the change, will be willing to co-operate with the centralized education system (those in authority) in the future. The teachers were humiliated by the system which viewed them as potential cheaters and untrustworthy, forcing them out of their own classrooms during the test and failing to brief them on what their students were expected to know. It is, after all, the teachers who will be asked to co-operate in 'correcting' the various reading comprehension problems detected on the tests. One wonders also about the message conveyed to students when their teachers are not trusted by the system.

An act of frightening and deterrence

The reading comprehension test was introduced to 'shake up' the instructional system. This goal of shaking up the system was not approached through the introduction of a new curriculum or a new teacher training programme but rather through the introduction of a test.

The Ministry employed various techniques to enhance fear and ensure that the introduction of the test did in fact shake the system. Before the administration of the test the Ministry of Education used the strategy of withholding information – that is, not making information about the test available to teachers and students; it refused to release any information about the test, the format, the questions, or its purpose. Withholding information, not unexpectedly, created tension, anger and anxiety. One reason that teachers were asked to leave the classroom was to maintain the secrecy of questions, thus allowing the same test to be used the following year. Keeping information from the public is the same strategy often used by teachers, when they withhold information about tests from their students and thus exercise power and control. Absence of information about the test is a device testers use to impose power and control.

Conclusions

Clearly, while the intended purpose of the test, as shown in the letter to the parents, was very educational, serving an acceptable code of confidentiality and ethicality, the reality is that a national test of this sort had major effects and consequences on education and society. The effects went far beyond what was stated in the official letter and probably far beyond what those who introduced the test could foresee. Clearly, this high-stake test had the effect of changing the behaviour of all those affected by its results, in terms of a number of specific domains in the educational system – materials, textbooks, allocation of classroom teaching time, interpretation of scores and attitudes. Yet even when the intention is educational, changes in behaviour take place far beyond those intended.

All the mechanisms of power described by Foucault operated within this examination, as the effects were far beyond teaching and learning. This occurred in a number of directions – causing the humiliation of teachers as well as other moral and ethical violations. Thus a test, because of its power, became a disciplinary tool capable of changing behaviours as well as leading to a variety of unethical actions. It is therefore evident here that, even with the best intentions, high-stake tests have major effects on a variety of factors and on the educational system in general. The Ministry, or those who are in charge of introducing the test, often do not examine such effects. Thus, it is the case that testers choose either not to enquire about the effects of tests or to turn their heads the other way so not to observe them. Yet, as this study showed, these types of effect exist. It is important that the tester weighs the cost of introducing tests in terms of their effects and consequences with regard to teaching and learning as well as the moral and ethical consequences of tests. While it was assumed here that the policy makers introducing the test were not aware of such effects, this is still an open question, given the difficulty of obtaining any data on the covert reasons for introducing the test. The data in this study did not include information on the undeclared rationale for introducing the test. The test, therefore, was probably introduced with the best educational intentions; yet, at the same time, it becomes evident that decision makers who introduce tests should be aware of the unintended and unexpected consequences, and study them so that such unethical consequences as were reported here can be avoided. The study that is discussed in the next chapter describes the introduction of a test for the specific intention of causing a change in behaviour.

9

An Arabic test

The context

This chapter reports on the intentions and effects of a test of Arabic as a second language. In Israel, Arabic is taught to Hebrew speakers as a second language (see also Shohamy, 1993, 1997, 1998; Shohamy *et al.*, 1996), given the large number of Arabs living in Israel (close to 20 per cent) as well as Arabic being a language of the Middle East. In addition, for about half of the Israeli population Arabic is a heritage language, as they immigrated to Israel from Arabic-speaking countries. Arabic is now a compulsory subject for most Hebrew speakers in Israel and there is strong encouragement to teach it. Yet, given the political conflict between Israel and the Arabs, the Arabic language is of very low status and there is no motivation among Hebrew speakers to study it (Ben-Rafael and Brosh, 1991; Shohamy and Donitsa-Schmidt, 1998). It is important, therefore, to understand the introduction of the Arabic test within the context of the role and status of Arabic in Israel.

From the beginning of the introduction of the test, statements made by the national inspector of Arabic, who was responsible for introducing the test, made it clear that measuring the level of Arabic was a method of imposing a change in the status and role of the Arabic language. The introduction of the test was a classic example of using a test to gain respect, and thus upgrade the status of a subject suffering from low prestige and low motivation on the part of students. In addition, the test was introduced to create a change in teaching habits and methods, operating under the assumption that only what is tested is valued and respected.

Background

The Arabic test was introduced by the Ministry of Education for seventh-, eighth- and ninth-grade students learning Arabic as a foreign language. The test was first administered in 1988 for seventh-grade students only; it is currently administered in the middle of each school year to all three grades. The Arabic curriculum for the seventh grade includes the teaching of the alphabet, grammatical structures, and a vocabulary of about 300 words; the eighth- and ninth-grade curricula both add about 300 new words each year.

Intentions

The intention behind introducing the test, according to the Arabic inspector at the Ministry of Education, was specifically to raise the prestige of the Arabic language, to motivate teachers to speed up their teaching of Arabic, to increase the motivation of both teacher and students, and to compare the levels of teaching of Arabic in schools throughout the country (Shohamy, Donitsa-Schmidt and Ferman 1996). Clearly, the Ministry of Education felt the study of Arabic needed a 'push' and that the test could provide a useful instrument for providing it.

One specific goal for introducing the seventh-grade test was to reduce the amount of time the teacher spent on teaching the alphabet. Previously, it had taken teachers about two years to teach the alphabet. The national inspector of Arabic believed that this was too long and should be reduced to six months. The administration of the test was therefore scheduled for six months after the beginning of the school year (during the month of March). The seventh-grade test included items that required letter recognition, vocabulary, and grammar. In the first few years of the administration of the test, the inspector distributed a vocabulary list from which the test vocabulary was selected.

In the case of the Arabic test, the inspector of Arabic publicly declared that the test was introduced for purposes other than measuring students' achievements. Specifically, it was introduced to:

- raise the prestige of the Arabic language
- standardize the levels of teaching Arabic
- increase the rate of teaching of the Arabic alphabet
- increase the motivation of teachers to teach and students to learn.

Effects

The effect of the test was examined in three separate yet related studies, at three different points in time. The first study examined the impact of the introduction of the test on teaching by comparing its effect before the test had been administered, with its effect after administration (Shohamy, 1993). The second study examined the effect of the test after it had been in the system for three years. The third study examined its long-range effect after it had been in the system for eight years (Shohamy, Donitsa-Schmidt and Ferman, 1996). The results of each of these studies are reported below.

Study 1: Effect of the test at introduction

The research questions in this study were mostly concerned with specific washback effects on teaching and learning. Thus, the following questions were posed regarding the Arabic test:

- How did the introduction of the test affect teaching practices?
- How did the introduction of the test affect students' behaviour?
- What was the long-range impact of the test?

To answer the first question, data were collected through class observations, reviews of teaching materials, interviews with teachers and questionnaires to students. Questionnaires were collected on two separate occasions: one to four weeks before the test, and one to two weeks following it. Observations were conducted in seventh-, eighth- and ninth-grade Arabic classes taught by different teachers. Each class was observed three times: twice before the test, and once following it. Each observation was followed by an interview with the teacher and an analysis of the teaching material. The number of students in each class ranged from 39 to 42. The focus of the observation was teaching activities associated with the test.

Teaching activities *before* the administration of the test

Observations prior to the administration of the test revealed that class time and activities were dominated by it; there were constant references to 'the test' and it had become the central focus and goal of all classroom activities. Typical of these lessons were review and preparation sessions with clear goals in terms of outcomes. Specifically, only material known to be on the test was discussed; any deviation from this was considered a diversion and a waste of time. The teachers were fully aware of this and explained that if they continued with 'regular' teaching, they would not have enough time to prepare their students for the test and the students would fail. The review period lasted between four and six weeks.

The following describes the main activities during the review period before the test was administered. The typical characteristic of the period was that teachers consciously stopped teaching *new* material and turned to *reviewing* materials. This meant that they stopped using the class textbooks, as they believed that the textbooks did not provide a good basis for the review because they did not cover the same material that was included in the test. They therefore produced worksheets which were essentially 'clones' of the previous year's test and used these worksheets during the review period. The worksheets primarily included long lists of words, sometimes up to 300, accompanied by translations. The word lists were used for all classes, while a list of the alphabet was used for the seventh grade.

Not only was the material test-like but the teaching activities were also test-like. These included teaching vocabulary in a decontextualized manner, using the word lists accompanied by their translations. There was ample use of repetition, rote practice, and mechanical grammar exercises while the learning of new material took place only when it was needed for the test, and this was done in a rush. There was no error correction, very little explanation of material, no checks as to whether the students had internalized or mastered the new material or if they could use it in different contexts; it was mostly mechanical rote learning. There were quick shifts from one topic to another; the impression was that quantity must come at the expense of quality, since there was so much to cover in so little time. Most of these activities were clones of the test, assigned after the teacher had explained the material briefly in class, and tests were used extensively for teaching material that had not been taught before.

Students were assigned homework which included activities that were 'more of the same'. This meant that the activities were mostly designed to allow students to complete at home what could not be covered during class time. There were also review sessions that lasted up to two hours a week and were added to regular class hours.

In terms of the language used in the classroom, there was extensive use of Hebrew as teachers claimed that using Arabic was a waste of time. The atmosphere in class was tense among both students and teachers. Yet, students were highly motivated to master the material, and no discipline problems were recorded as students felt there were clear goals for learning.

Teaching activities *after* the administration of the test

Observations conducted after the administration of the test showed no reference at all to 'the test', and regular teaching was resumed. Specifically, new material was taught mostly through textbooks. The vocabulary was taught in a contextualized manner, usually through stories and conversations, and language was introduced through communicative activities such as teachers' personal stories, discussions and pictures. There was substantially less homework but it was more varied and contextualized. No tests were used throughout the whole observation period in any of the classes. In terms of the language used in the classroom, there was much more Arabic than Hebrew and the class atmosphere was more relaxed as the pace was slower. However, it also seemed to be less efficient and some discipline problems were noticed.

Table 9.1 Comparison of activities before and after the administration of the test

Before the test	After the test
Review of material	Teaching of new material
Use of worksheets	Use of textbooks
Isolated vocabulary lists	Contextualized vocabulary, via stories and conversations
Decontextualized teaching	Communicative/contextualized language
Rote learning, memorization, drills	Contextual, meaningful activities
Ample homework	Little homework
Use of L1	Use of L2
Frequent use of tests for teaching	No use of tests for teaching
Tense atmosphere	Relaxed atmosphere
Rushed pace	Slow pace
No discipline problems	Some discipline problems

Table 9.1 summarizes the differences between teaching activities *before* and *after* the test.

The following example illustrates some of the activities and the atmosphere in one class before and after the test. The description is based on three observations.

Observation 1 (before the test)

In the lesson that preceded this one, the teacher had distributed a vocabulary list of 300 words with their Hebrew translations. These words had been selected from the list of words for the test, and the students had been asked to memorize them at home. However, the students came to class unprepared and had not mastered those words. The teacher was angry, the students complained that it was too much to learn at one time, and the teacher complained that the students were lazy. The teacher started to test individual students orally, to prove that they did not know the words. As expected, the students did not know the words, and they were upset and tense. The teacher gave them an assignment to prepare for a test on the same vocabulary for the next lesson; the test would include 100 of the words. The students had to memorize the words on their own; no teaching of vocabulary took place.

Observation 2 (five days later, before the test)

The teacher returned the tests that had been administered in the previous lessons (not observed). The teacher stated that 90 per cent of the students had failed the test and accused the students of not studying hard enough. She tested them again, orally, by inviting individual students to the board to correct words that were wrong on the test. The teacher dictated the words and asked students to translate them as part of class work, while she went around the classroom checking each student's work.

Observation 3 (one week after the test)

The atmosphere was relaxed, the teacher was calm. Students were asked to open their books to a new story. The teacher read new vocabulary lists, read a text that included the words and held a discussion on the content of the study utilizing the new words. This activity lasted until the end of the session. The teacher did not translate any of the new words (of which there were 20), and there was frequent use of L2. However, not all the students participated, and some were bored; there were some discipline problems and the teacher admitted later (in the interview) that there had been lack of attention and a decrease in motivation since the administration of the test.

In summary, an examination of the effect of the test on teaching practice showed that there was a sharp distinction between teaching and testing: teaching stopped, and test review began. There was constant reference to the test, and all activities were geared to it. No new material was taught during the review period, except for topics needed for the test. There was ample use of worksheets, homework and tests as preparation devices. The main goal was to succeed on the test. After the test was administered, learning of new material resumed. Teaching consisted of contextualized and communicative activities and the use of L2. Compared with the period before the test, the lessons were less focused and less efficient.

Effect of the test on students

Data on the effect of the test on students were collected through questionnaires administered to 45 students and from the above-mentioned classroom observations.

While 45 per cent of the students claimed that the test had not affected them, 55 per cent claimed that it did in fact have an effect. Those who claimed to have been affected said that the test made them listen more carefully during lessons, pay more attention to the subject, and take Arabic studies more seriously. It motivated them to learn and to take private tutoring to make up for missed material.

In terms of the type of impact, 62 per cent claimed that the test affected them *positively*, while 38 per cent claimed that it had affected them *negatively*. Those who claimed to have been affected positively said that the test forced them to learn more Arabic, enriched their knowledge of the subject matter, improved their grades, helped them to master new vocabulary, enriched their language and motivated their learning.

Those who claimed to have been affected negatively by the test claimed that the test introduced fear, pressure and anxiety and frustrated them, since they felt that the test did not reflect their real learning. It gave them a feeling of wasted time and it did not contribute to improved proficiency in Arabic.

Thus, different students were affected by the test in different ways. For some it was beneficial, for others it was not. All students claimed that they learned more because the material was more focused. They felt that they had a better idea of what was expected of them in learning Arabic, as the test focused their learning.

In conclusion, the Arabic test was a low-stake test in that the results had no sanctioning power in a subject considered to be of low prestige. Yet, the test was powerful enough to change the behaviour of all teachers and of most of the students. However, it is clear from this study that such an effect was limited to the teaching and learning that took place before the administration of the test. In this period teachers stopped teaching the regular material, replaced the textbooks with test-like worksheets and increased the use of tests and quizzes in class. But once the test had been administered, teachers switched to 'regular teaching'. Thus, the effects associated with the power of the test, in terms of it being a disciplinary tool capable of changing the behaviour of others, are limited to a period when the vision of the test is clear.

Study 2: Impact of the test after three years

The effect of the test after it had been in operation for three years was examined by collecting data that focused on the seventh grade only, since for that grade there was an explicit goal of shortening the amount of time required for teaching the Arabic alphabet. Thus, one type of impact examined was the extent to which that goal was achieved. Other questions that were examined related to whether the teachers used the test content in teaching; whether the test affected teaching methods; whether it changed teachers' perceptions of Arabic as a school subject; and whether it changed the status of Arabic as a school subject.

The data were collected from 12 teachers of Arabic from various parts of the country, whose seventh-grade classes were tested. Questionnaires were completed, personal interviews were held, and their classes were observed. The questionnaires consisted of 16 questions that addressed aspects of the test's impact on teaching methods and the perception of Arabic as a school subject. Four of the questions focused on the teacher's background, six on teaching and testing methods, and six on perception of Arabic as a school subject. In addition, interviews were conducted with each of the teachers, to validate the responses obtained from the questionnaires. Classroom observations were aimed at finding out whether there were overt or covert references to the test and to examine the specific activities in which teachers were engaged before the administration of the test. In addition, students' notebooks were reviewed.

The results of the questionnaire showed that half of the teachers reported that they were affected by the test and that it influenced their teaching, while the other half reported that the test had no influence on their teaching. However, as it turned out, all those claiming not to have been influenced were new teachers who had recently graduated from teacher-training institutions, where they had been trained in teaching the alphabet in a shorter amount of time. All the teachers who claimed to have been influenced by the test had been teaching for more than five years.

Those who claimed to have been influenced by the test reported that the test gave them direction as to the setting of new teaching priorities: it affected their allocation of time causing them to reduce the amount of lessons devoted to teaching the alphabet, and created pressure and tension as it interrupted their regular teaching. Yet, at the same time they felt that the test gave them direction as to what aspects of Arabic needed to be taught, and how. They also admitted that they felt that the test upgraded the status of Arabic as a subject.

The results of classroom observations performed before and after the test showed that there was very little special preparation for the test, since the new textbooks being used were a direct reflection of the test. The most apparent impact of the test was the development of new textbooks, based on new approaches to teaching the alphabet and including the same activities that were on the test. Thus, while in the early years of the test there was a distinct difference between teaching and testing, that difference became blurred over time, as new textbooks that reflected the test appeared on the market. Thus, by the time of this study the alphabet was in fact taught in a substantially shorter amount of time. In terms of vocabulary, teaching consisted mostly of the words included on the test. Thus, over the years teachers have begun to teach Arabic in the 'new way', geared to the test. The gap between testing and teaching has therefore diminished as the two have become integrated. The new textbooks have become, de facto, the new curriculum.

In conclusion, when the new Arabic test was first introduced, there was a strong immediate test effect as teaching stopped and test preparation began. The material needed for the test became the body of knowledge to be mastered. The preparation for that body of knowledge became instrumental as students and teachers knew what they wanted to achieve. Activities became very focused and efficient, covering only material known to be in the test. Thus learning became narrow, mechanical and superficial; it was expressed through 'test-like' activities such as worksheets that replicated the test in terms of form and content, review materials, special lessons preparing students for the test, and a large dose of testing and quizzes. That strong impact of the test lasted approximately four to six weeks; afterwards, teaching returned to the non-test format. However, as time went by, after a period of three years, teaching and testing had become synonymous. This was mainly as a result of the introduction of the new textbooks designed to match the new body of knowledge – the test material. These textbooks were clones of the test, especially in terms of their activities and tasks; they became the new teaching material. Testing and teaching became quite similar, very few review sessions were observed, and teachers admitted to having been influenced by the test in terms of direction and guidance. The Ministry of Education was therefore successful in introducing new material through the device of a test. Thus, in the long run, the disciplinary power of the test was expanded to other components of the education system – to textbooks, teaching methods and to the teaching material. The test was thus capable of influencing a whole system.

How did the test, which was of low stake, become so influential? The main reason is that the teaching of Arabic is very much in its preliminary phases. There is still much confusion surrounding what is best practice. In such situations, when there is lack of pedagogical knowledge, the inspectorate and the central authorities responsible for giving directions in the field are very powerful. They clearly used the test to communicate to the field specific pedagogical priorities – what should be taught, how quickly it should be carried out, etc. In situations when pedagogical knowledge is minimal, the test becomes the substitute for other ways of communication such as curriculum, in-service training, etc.

Study 3: The long-range impact of the test

Since the initial administration of the test, it has become routine practice in the Israeli education system. It was therefore of interest to examine the long-range effect of the test and whether the impact it had had in the previous studies still persists (Shohamy, Donitsa-Schmidt and Ferman, 1996).

The Arabic test has become an integral part of the teaching of Arabic. Every year around March the test is administered to all the ASL students in the country. Over the years some changes have taken place:

1. The administration of the test has extended from grades 7–9 to grades 10, 11 and 12.
2. A reading comprehension component has been added.
3. Options for the inclusion of the testing of listening comprehension and Arabic culture have been added.

The rationale behind these changes, according to the Arabic inspectorate, was to maintain a basic standard of achievement in all grade levels, to provide an up-to-date diagnostic picture of students' achievements, and to integrate reading and listening comprehension as basic skills with less emphasis on grammar (Arabic as a Second Language, *Teachers' Journal*, August, 1994). The methods and results of this study are explained below.

Method

The sample of the study included teachers, students and inspectors. Specifically, nine ASL teachers of grades 7–11, 62 ASL students of grades 7–11 randomly selected from ten different classes, and two ASL inspectors – one a national inspector and the other regional.

Three types of *instrument* were used for collecting the data:

1. *Questionnaires*, administered to students and addressing the following variables: awareness of the test; allotment of time to teaching activities; time spent on preparation for the test; attitudes towards the effect of the test on learning; and views concerning test quality. Some 24 Likert scale items were used (some ranging from 1 to 5, others from 1 to 3) and eight open-ended questions.
2. *Structured interviews* were held with teachers and inspectors. These included questions regarding preparation for the test; awareness of the test among students, teachers, school principals and parents; impact of the test on various aspects such as teaching and testing practices; available courseware, attitudes of students and school administration towards learning and towards the tests; and views concerning test quality.
3. *Document analysis* of the Director General Bulletins (1984–96) and instructions used by the Ministry of Education Inspectorate concerning the tests. In addition, material received by teachers and testers from the inspectorate was analysed, as was new courseware intended for teaching and copies of the ASL teachers' journals.

The data were collected in 1995, three months prior to the administration of the test. The questionnaires were administered to the students of ASL during class time. The administration took about 15 minutes and was preceded by a brief introduction assuring students of confidentiality. The interviews with the teachers and inspectors were held on a one-to-one basis. Each interview lasted for about one hour. All interviews were recorded and then transcribed.

Results

The results of the effect of the test were analysed according to the following nine dimensions: (a) effect of the test on classroom activities and time allotment; (b) teaching material; (c) awareness of the test; (d) perceived effects of the test results; (e) status of subject and skill tested; (f) perception of the quality of the test; (g) perception of the test's importance; (h) impact of test on promoting learning; and (i) impact of the test as perceived by bureaucrats.

(a) *Effect of the test on classroom activities and time allotment*

It was found that there had been very little preparation for the test in terms of class activities and time spent. All nine teachers reported that they did not inform their students about the tests and did not allot any special time for preparation.

Specifically, teachers stated that, unlike in previous years, they no longer gave lists of words for the students to memorize nor did they prepare any special drills for the test. Furthermore, they did not notify students beforehand when the test would take place, and did not teach for the test or review material that would be included in the test. They basically continued to use the textbook that had been used during the school year, did not prepare any special material for the test such as previous years' tests for review, drills and format of the test, and did not add extra review hours. In terms of atmosphere, there was no tension in the class concerning the exam.

Two teachers added that they regarded the test merely as a quiz. Teachers stated that since the test had been administered for nine years by then, they were already familiar with the test routine and types of drill included in it. Consequently, they tended to include these types of drill throughout the school year in order to familiarize the students with them. Teachers also added that they did not prepare for the test, as such preparation disturbs the fluency of teaching and sequence of the curriculum material.

According to the students' questionnaires, 86 per cent indicated that there were no special activities in class prior to the administration of the test. Some 72 per cent reported that no time at all was devoted in class to the test. In an open-ended question, students noted that teaching was conducted as usual and 'we don't devote any time to special activities for the test'.

(b) Teaching material

In terms of teaching material generated by the ASL test, it was found – according to interviews with teachers, inspectors and documents analysis – that no special courseware of the ASL test had been published since 1993.

(c) Awareness of the test

Results showed that there was very low awareness of the existence and content of the test among students and their parents. In fact, 63 per cent of the students declared in the questionnaires that they did not know of the existence of the test. Moreover, 90 per cent of the students did not know what material the test covers. In addition, 77 per cent of the students said that their parents did not know about the test. The results are in line with teachers' statements that they did not inform their classes of the test.

(d) Perceived effects of the test results

While teachers do not attach any significant consequences to the test, most students do. Results show that although all nine Arabic teachers firmly rejected the idea that the grade of the national test will be taken into consideration in the students' final year, 52 per cent of the students thought that the test grade would affect their final grade in Arabic to a large extent and 62 per cent claimed that the test would affect their knowledge of Arabic and future success in their studies.

Another issue teachers raised in relation to the lack of any effect of test results is the absence of diagnostic feedback resulting from the test and lack of information regarding the standing of the class in comparison with other classes and schools. Once the test is over, the test event is forgotten since there appear to be no consequences.

(e) *Status of subject and skill tested*

All teachers agreed that the test has not changed any of the students' attitudes towards Arabic and that the low prestige of this subject has remained unchanged. Seven out of the nine Arabic teachers claimed that the test has not raised the status of Arabic in school. They claimed that they did not change their attitude or behaviour because of the national test. Furthermore, the Arabic lessons, as well as the test, were not given any priorities over other activities.

In answer to a question about whether the test increases the subject's prestige, 67 per cent of students answered 'not at all'. Some 65 per cent stated that they do not find it important to succeed in this test for such reasons as: 'It is a test the purpose of which is to get a national profile and not a personal profile'; 'Students are not tested on the class material and the grade is not included in the final grade at the end of the school year'.

(f) *Perception of the quality of the test*

Both teachers and students complained that the test was of poor quality. All nine teachers stated that the test was neither valid nor reliable for the following reasons:

- The material tested did not necessarily match the material studied during the school year.
- The material included less reading comprehension and more grammar and translation drills.
- Test results did not depict a true picture of their students' knowledge in Arabic.

All Arabic teachers stated that the test should be re-evaluated and revised, and all expressed negative feelings towards it. In line with teachers' complaints, 64 per cent of the students reported that the test did not reflect their true knowledge of Arabic.

(g) *Perception of the test's importance*

Teachers and students expressed negative feelings toward the test and complained that the test was of no importance and not essential in all class levels. The upper level teachers expressed dissatisfaction with the fact that the Ministry of Education found it necessary to test high school achievement. 'After all,' said one teacher, 'our students are geared towards the end of high school matriculation exam, so it is obvious that teaching occurs and that teachers are doing their best to prepare their students for the final exam without the need to be constantly reminded of it by administering an external exam.'

Teachers agreed that it was important to go on administering the test in the lower level classes but not in the higher classes, since the teaching of Arabic in the lower level was compulsory and thus the learning was more effective with the 'threat and power' of the test behind it. In the higher levels – high school classes – Arabic studies are optional and there is no need to use a test as a forcing and threatening device.

(h) *Impact of test on promoting learning*

All those teaching the upper-level classes insisted that the test did not promote learning in the upper grades, since students were committed to learning the subject without the need of external intervention. The lower grade teachers, on the other hand, were more positive and said that the test may have had some effect in promoting the learning, although they could not be certain of that.

All teachers complained that the Ministry of Education was trying to promote learning by introducing and forcing new material into the test and thus expecting teachers to teach it. Teachers rejected the possibility that such methods would effectively promote learning, since no training had been given on how to teach the new components.

(i) *Impact of the test as perceived by bureaucrats*

The Arabic inspectors were aware of the fact that, in previous years, test anxiety was high among teachers and students, and that there had been a decrease in test anxiety and fear of sanctions. The inspectors were also aware of the fact that some teachers did not administer the Arabic test at all, or treated it as a quiz for which no preparation was needed. They stated, however, that although there were still problems with the test it was essential that it continue to be administered, as they believed that there would be a major and significant drop in the level of Arabic proficiency in the country if the test were cancelled. Moreover, the inspectorate claimed that there would be a decrease in the number of students studying Arabic, since the test promoted the status of Arabic as perceived by teachers, students and parents.

Conclusions

In examining the consequences of the Arabic test after a number of years, based on the three studies, certain findings emerge.

In the first study, conducted when the test was introduced, the power of the test was capable of changing the behaviour of teachers and learners, but only as long as the test was in sight – immediately before the administration of the test.

In the second study, after three years the test had a much broader impact; it was capable of changing the whole domain of teaching Arabic, as the test content was in fact integrated into all the domains – curriculum, teaching and learning. Yet this is probably due to the specific vacuum in pedagogical knowledge. The test then provided the source of knowledge, substituting for other, more beneficial sources such as teacher training and revised curriculum. These are the situations when tests are most powerful, their effect is most noticed and they are capable of changing educational behaviours most significantly.

In the third study, after the test had been in operation for eight years and had become a routine procedure, it was possible to examine whether the intentions and goals of the inspector when introducing the test were achieved. The results show that while the test managed to change the specific teaching procedures, it did not fulfil any of the inspector's agendas beyond teaching methods. It did not raise the status and level of the subject, nor did it increase the number of students learning Arabic (an indication of its prestige).

Yet the inspector insisted that the test must continue to be administered every year. He feared that if the test were cancelled there would be a drop in the national level of Arabic proficiency and a decrease in the number of students studying it, claiming that the test promotes the status of Arabic as viewed by teachers, students and parents. Clearly, as its main impact the test provided the inspector with a disciplinary tool. This provided a feeling of bureaucratic power and control over the system, with an illusion of action – and most probably an excuse for not taking meaningful pedagogical actions. Some claim this may have been the main reason for introducing the test in the first place.

10

An English test

The context

Unlike Arabic, which is a language of low status in the schools system and society, English benefits from a very high status, often claimed to have a higher status and prestige than Hebrew. English – being the world's current lingua franca, the method of communication with the outside world – is a language that is needed for obtaining successful jobs, promotions, academic functioning and business interactions. A knowledge of the English language is considered in Israel as an indicator of success, to the point that a working proficiency in English is a prequisite for entrance to most workplaces and universities. All children and parents realize this and have very positive attitudes and motivations towards the study of English. Children start taking private English lessons at a very early age and schools are offering English at a younger and younger age – at the moment in third grade, although many schools offer English as early as the first grade. Thus, tests of the English language have a very different status to those of Arabic or of reading comprehension. Passing the English tests at a high grade almost guarantees belonging to the upper segment of society. The English test is consequently a very high-stake test. It is interesting, therefore, to find out what the expectations and intentions of decision makers are in introducing English tests and what effects these tests have on the definition of the English language and its learning and teaching. Given the high status of the subject and the power of those who master English, it is to be expected that it will have a strong effect on learning. But at the same time, decision makers will use it for promoting curricular agendas.

This chapter reports on two studies that examined the effects and consequences of an English as a Foreign Language (EFL) oral proficiency test used for graduation from secondary school (see Shohamy, 1993, 1997, 1998; Shohamy et al., 1996). The first study examined the effect of the oral test when it was first introduced in 1986. The second study examined the effect of a modified version of the oral test incorporated into the education system ten years later, in 1996.

Study 1: intentions and effects of an EFL oral test

Background

The EFL oral test is part of the national matriculation examination, administered at the end of 12th grade to all students graduating from high school. A new oral test was introduced in 1986 after a series of experiments (Shohamy, Reves and Bejarano, 1986). It consisted of a number of tasks representing the following speech interactions: oral interviews, role plays, reporting, picture descriptions and literature. The test was administered to individual students, in two separate stations, by different testers. The first station consisted of an oral interview and a role play; the second consisted of a picture description and the literature test. Each station lasted about seven minutes. The oral test that preceded this test, consisted of an unstructured oral interview that was similar to a conversation.

Intentions

The main intentions for introducing the new oral test in 1986, as explained by the chief inspector of English at the time, were to increase the emphasis on oral language in the EFL classroom, to make teachers teach oral language and thus to upgrade the speaking proficiency of high school graduating students. Using the *Bagrut* (end of secondary school examination) to influence the high school curriculum has been a consistent policy in the teaching of English as well as other subjects in the secondary curriculum. In that education system the examinations became the method of asserting power over the teaching. The chief inspector admitted that 'the most effective way of ensuring that the aims of a curriculum are indeed carried out is through the final school-leaving examination' (Gefen, 1983). Thus the Bagrut became the 'unofficial syllabus'. 'Putting something in the examination one year can ensure that it will be taught the next year' (Horovitz, 1986). After a year of trial, a new oral examination, with two external examiners and involving an interview, a monologue, a role play and an oral literature test – all marked using a rating scale – came into effect in 1986.

Effects

Method

The effects of the new oral test on the teaching of spoken English in the classroom were examined via data collected from observations, and interviews, with 15 teachers – ten teachers with up to five years' experience and five new teachers. The main findings are described below.

Time spent on oral language

All the experienced teachers claimed that the test affected their behaviour in the sense that they spent substantially more time on oral language in the classroom than they had done before the new test was introduced. Five of the teachers claimed to have spent no time at all on oral language before the test was introduced. The novice teachers – those who had taught for up to three years – claimed that the test did not affect their behaviour, since they had been trained in the teaching of oral language at their teacher-training institutions.

Classroom activities

As to the specific class activities used to teach oral language, it was found that they were identical to the activities included on the test – class interviews, role plays, picture descriptions and reports. No other activities were observed or reported in the interviews. The tendency may have been reinforced by a booklet published by the Ministry of Education in preparation for the test, which included lists of topics and role plays. This booklet was designed to ease the transition from the old to the new oral testing system. It provided a source from which teachers could draw specific activities for practising for the test.

With regard to how teachers perceived oral language, the findings showed that they perceived it exclusively in terms of test-like activities. Thus, when asked to define 'oral language proficiency' teachers often gave answers such as 'It is the ability to role play in the language' or 'It is an interview'.

Experienced vs novice teachers

There were major differences between experienced and novice teachers with regard to the influence of the test. The new teachers tended to try out more test-like activities in the teaching of oral language. For example, they undertook a variety of communicative activities in their classes such as debates, simulations, lectures, plays, discussions and group activities. They claimed that having this type of test actually opened new teaching avenues to them and, therefore, they experimented with innovative types of interactions. The difference between novice and experienced teachers is probably due to the fact that the novice teachers had been trained in oral language teaching in their teacher-training programmes and were therefore familiar with a variety of methods for teaching oral language. The experienced teachers, on the other hand, who had not received such training, turned to the test as their main source of guidance for teaching oral language. They viewed the oral test as an additional burden they had to deal with in order to prepare their students for the test, and they took the shortest possible route to that goal.

It is clear that the test did have an impact and was instrumental in diverting attention to what had not been explicitly taught previously. The EFL oral test actually made teachers devote more time to, and place greater emphasis on, oral language in the classroom. It is interesting to note that the test content had been included in the curriculum prior to the test, though not in the specific manner the Ministry of Education wanted it to be taught; English oral language had been taught through other subjects or though general literacy. Through the introduction of the test, the Ministry of Education successfully imposed the teaching of specific topics that it considered important. Students found the test to be helpful in clarifying goals and for learning.

Yet, in terms of the nature of the input, the results showed that instruction became test-like. This was found both in teaching methods and materials created. In this case, the teaching of oral language in the classroom became test-like, in that it involved specific activities and tasks that were included in the test and had not been practised previously.

It is also interesting to note that the use of test-like activities is most likely to be a result of teachers not having been trained to teach the new areas being tested. Without appropriate pedagogical knowledge, teachers turned to the most immediate and readily available features – the test. Thus, in a situation where the educational leadership did not provide experienced teachers with on-the-job training in new areas, teachers turned to the test as their single source of knowledge regarding methods of instruction.

Conclusions

The declared purpose for introducing the test, as stated by the EFL Inspector, was to divert teachers' attention to the teaching of oral language – an area believed by the Inspectorate to be overlooked – and the study showed that the goal had been achieved. Teachers, indeed, spent substantially more time teaching oral language, yet the teaching included only the specific tasks that appeared on the test, namely interviews, monologue and role plays. It was therefore 'oral test language', substantially narrower than the 'oral language' that had been taught and became the *de facto* oral knowledge.

Study 2: Intentions and effects of the modified oral test

This study examined the intentions and impact of the modified oral test which was introduced by 1996 into the Israeli education system (Shohamy, Donitse-Schmidt and Ferman, 1996).

Background

The EFL oral test has become a routine procedure in the teaching of English since 1986. Over the years it has undergone a number of modifications. The first change took place in 1994 when the Ministry of Education stipulated that instead of two external examiners, students would be tested by one external and one internal examiner, their own teacher. A number of changes were due to take place in the summer of 1996 and were announced in a bulletin of the Ministry of Education. The changes were as follows:

- An extensive reading part will be added in which students report on two books they will have read by the time of the test. A reading file will be prepared by the pupil and handed to the teacher one month before the oral test.
- The traditional role play will be replaced by a 'modified' role play, where students ask the tester a series of questions based on forms and cue cards.
- The interview and monologue will be replaced by an extended interview.
- The rating scales which measure accuracy and fluency will be changed slightly and a new scale of task orientation will be added.
- The literature part remains unchanged.

Intentions

The rationale and intentions for introducing the modified version of the test, as stated by the EFL English Inspectorate were '. . . to provide an opportunity for authentic speech and communication and to gauge the pupil's overall level of oral proficiency' (Steiner, 1995: 15). The aim was to encourage pupils to read:

> It is important to see the Reading for Pleasure program as a process, and not as an end-product on the day of the oral matriculation exam. It is a process that should start in elementary school and continue up through all grade levels.
>
> (Steiner, 1995: 2)

A further intention was 'to encourage students to read, to provide an opportunity for authentic speech and communication and to gauge the pupils' overall level of oral proficiency' (Steiner, 1995: 15).

Effects

Method

The effect of the test was examined in the following way. The *sample* included teachers, students and inspectors: 16 teachers of EFL in grades 9–12; 50 EFL students ranging from grades 9 to 12 who were randomly selected from a large sample of 200 students, from 10 different classes; and four EFL national and regional inspectors.

Three data collection procedures were used:

(a) Questionnaires administered to students addressing the following variables: awareness of the test; allotment of time to teaching activities; time spent on preparation for the test; attitudes towards the effect of the test on learning; and views concerning test quality. Twenty-four Likert scale items were used (some ranging from 1 to 5, others from 1 to 3) and eight open-ended questions.

(b) Structured interviews were held with teachers and inspectors. These included questions regarding preparation for the test; awareness of the test among students, teachers, school principals and parents; impact of the test on various aspects such as teaching and testing practices; available courseware; attitudes of students and school administration towards learning and towards the tests; and views concerning test quality.

(c) Analyses of various documents – the Director General Bulletins (1984–96) and instructions issued by the Ministry of Education Inspectorate concerning the tests. In addition, material received by teachers and testers from the Inspectorate was analysed, as was new courseware intended for teaching and copies of the ESL teachers' journals.

Results

As with the Arabic test reported in the previous chapter, the results of the effect of the test were analysed according to the following nine dimensions: (a) the effect of the test on classroom activities and time allotment; (b) teaching materials; (c) awareness of the test; (d) perceived effects of the test results; (e) the status of the subject and skills tested; (f) perception of test quality; (g) perception of the test's importance; (h) impact of the test on promoting learning; and (i) impact of the test as perceived by bureaucrats.

(a) Classroom activities and time allotment

Based on teachers' interviews, it was found that the test affects teaching in terms of content as well as methodology. Teachers added that their way of teaching for the current examination is based on their previous experience since almost no training has been provided by the English Inspectorate on the method of teaching. Teachers reported using specific teaching activities in preparation for the test.

The eight teachers of the upper level (whose students were due to take the test in 1996) claimed to focus their teaching exclusively on the oral skills to be tested: interviewing, speaking at length, asking questions, discussing literature, reporting on books read and using reading files. These skills are being practised through simulations of test situations by a teacher and/or a peer. They also reported using techniques such as brainstorming, working in pairs, group discussions, speeches, etc. Teachers reported that they used the above practices in order to improve students' achievements in the oral test. Common reactions of the teachers to the impact that the test had on their method of teaching were: 'Of course I teach the tasks for the exam', 'I do exercises which simulate the exam', 'There is no alternative but to teach as dictated by the exam' and 'Does the exam affect my teaching? Oh sure, it has to!'.

On the other hand, the four lower-level teachers reported that they focus less on the specific skills to be tested, rather engaging in more creative types of oral activity such as class discussions, games, student talks and minilectures, student debating clubs, mini-plays and audio/video recordings. Common reactions were: 'I can be more creative as I am not pressured by the exam yet', 'My students know about the oral exam and we engage in activities like those tested in the exam, but also in other activities' and 'I can afford to spend time on a variety of oral activities as I am not preparing directly for the exam'.

Student responses in the questionnaires confirmed the above: 54.3 per cent of the upper-grade students reported intense preparation for the exam while only 13.3 per cent of the lower-level students reported this.

In terms of time allotment, the upper level teachers reported spending 1.5–2 hours a week for two years of studies (out of the five allotted for English) on preparation for the test: 'Sure, you make the time to deal with oral skills; otherwise [i.e., without the test], you would not.' Teachers reported tutoring students on an individual basis, mainly because some students cannot perform orally in front of the class and in order to decrease their test anxiety. Teachers reported that as the test date approached teaching became substantially intensified: 'I will spend much more time on oral activities a month or so before the exam' and 'I feel that not enough time has been spent on oral activities and I definitely need to work on the oral activities more intensively'. Teachers further reported that their students would be released from studies on the day of the test and for two days preceding it. The lower-level teachers, on the other hand, reported spending on average, close to one hour a week on oral activities: 'I spend about 20 per cent of each lesson engaging in oral activities' and 'On average about one weekly hour is dedicated to oral proficiency'.

Time allotment was reflected in students' questionnaires as follows: 74.3 per cent of the upper-grade students reported spending one hour a week or more on preparation for the oral examination while only 20 per cent of the lower-level students reported spending time on oral activities.

In terms of the impact of the test on teaching activities, teachers admitted that if the test were cancelled it would affect their way of teaching, as oral language would be taught to a much lesser degree and more time would be spent on teaching other language skills: 'We would go back to teaching written skills only', 'There would be no intentions to teach oral proficiency' and 'Teachers would focus on skills tested by the ministry and the oral skills would become just a by-product'.

(b) Teaching materials

Ample new material has been published and marketed since the announcement of the test changes became public. There is an abundance of both old and new teaching materials such as textbooks, audio/video cassettes and newspapers. Teachers were encouraged by the English Inspectorate to use the materials that have been published and marketed commercially, and are available, for preparation for the test. Not only did the courseware focus on the examination skills but there were also materials designed for specific oral skills tested in the examination, such as video cassettes and books designed for the teaching of literature, a TV series designed to teach extended speech, cue-cards and forms designed to teach the student to ask questions for the modified role play, an audio series of literary items tested in the oral examination and newspapers designed to prepare students for the extended interview.

(c) Awareness of the test

According to teachers' interviews, students were notified by their respective teachers of the pending changes for the 1996 oral test at the very beginning of the school year. They received detailed information with regard to the new format and content of the test and the rating scales. In fact, students' questionnaires show that 97.1 per cent of the upper-level students and 60 per cent of their parents are aware of the changes in the new EFL test.

(d) Perceived effects of the test results

Most of the teachers reported that the test created an atmosphere of high anxiety and fear of test results among teachers and students. Teachers felt that the success or failure of their students reflected on them and they spoke of pressure to cover the material for the test; one of the teachers referred to this issue as follows: 'The inspectors create pressure, informing us they could show up at any moment to check on us.'

Students' questionnaires reflected a similar picture: in terms of test anxiety, 96 per cent of the students reported being quite anxious about the test. Of all the students, 86 per cent believed that the test results could affect their overall matriculation score to a large extent and 70 per cent believed that the test results could affect their success in future studies.

(e) The status of the subject and skills tested

Teachers appreciated the status attached to the EFL oral test: 'The test gives oral proficiency an official status'. Ten out of 16 teachers interviewed reported that school administrators attribute high status value to the test, as demonstrated in the following practices:

- Teachers have been released from teaching duties in order to participate in conferences and workshops organized by the English Inspectorate as training session for the tests.
- Schools have allotted a special budget for photocopying materials required for preparation for the test.
- Schools have purchased additional extensive reading books for the school library.
- School administrators have instructed students to purchase extra books.

(f) Perception of test quality

All the EFL teachers reported negative attitudes towards the quality of the test; they viewed the test as neither valid nor reliable, listing the following reasons in the interviews:

- Oral testing on an individual basis is affected by a variety of factors which interact and eventually affect the student's scores, such as test anxiety and prejudices formed by the examiner prior to the test.
- The test is too short to reflect the student's level of oral proficiency.
- Testers are not professionals as insufficient training has been provided, e.g. they often ignore the objective rating scales provided by the English Inspectorate.
- The test procedure is based on testing situations which are not authentic enough.

Although the teachers criticized the test in its current form and found the logistics involved in its implementation very difficult, they approved of some of the changes made by the Inspectorate. For example, the class teacher being made the internal examiner and cancelling the role play and the monologue.

(g) Perception of the test's importance

Teachers realize the importance of the oral test and would not want the ministry to cancel it. Teachers stressed that they view the test as important, since it focuses on the communicative oral skills of English which are therefore taught to the students. One of the teachers stressed that these skills will be needed by the students in the future: 'Not all my students will need their English for academic purposes but they will all have to be able to speak in order to join the western world and take advantage of modern technology.'

Teachers were aware of the fact that students regard the oral exam as the most important criterion to evaluate their command of English. Students' questionnaires confirmed the above: 82 per cent of the students regarded the exam as very important; and 84 per cent of the students stated that it is of considerable importance to them to succeed on the oral exam. In an open-ended question, students referred to such reasons as: 'It is part of the official matriculation exam', 'It is an obligatory exam of the Ministry of Education', 'You cannot have a matriculation score in English without it' and 'This test shows your real knowledge of English'.

(h) *Impact of the test on promoting learning*

Teachers stated that the administration of the oral test had a considerable effect on focusing the attention of all those involved in oral proficiency. The promotion of teaching and learning oral skills was a direct result of the oral test administration. However, teachers claimed that not all parts of the oral test had a direct effect on promoting learning. Although teachers recognized the importance of extensive reading, they criticized the extensive reading part of the oral test in its current form, claiming that they had very little control over what their students had read (since students could make their own choices) or if they had read at all: 'I feel it is all sham', 'I don't really know what I am testing here', 'How on earth can I test students on books I myself haven't read?!' and 'I think this part of the test is really meaningless'. Teachers doubted if in its present form this part of the test could really promote reading, as many of the reading tasks were an incompetent way of promoting this skill. Moreover, teachers complained that insufficient training on the subject of the oral test had been given by the English Inspectorate.

With regard to the impact of the test on promoting learning, students' questionnaires indicated the following: 68 per cent of the students believed that testing promotes learning from quite a large to a very large degree; and 92 per cent of the students stated that the aim of the oral test was to promote the level of learning. With regard to the effect of the oral test on their command of English, 34 per cent believed that their command of English was affected by the test to a large extent while 46 per cent believed that there was little if any effect.

(i) *Impact of the test as perceived by bureaucrats*

The English Inspectorate claimed that the introduction of the oral test had a very positive educational impact and the washback on teaching had been tremendous. From an educational point of view, they stated that the oral test has been a great success and that expanding and emphasizing the oral skills had been achieved not only in the higher grades but also in the lower grades, although only the higher grades were being tested. The inspectors explained that the extensive reading components had been added in order to create a washback, which they believed could already be seen, as the reading files that the pupils had to prepare for the oral test have led students to read English not only in the upper-level grades but even in the lower-level grades. The English Inspectorate believed in the importance of the test and maintained that if the oral test was cancelled, teachers would cease teaching oral proficiency. The English Inspectorate admitted that very few training sessions were held on the method of testing – and none on the method of teaching for the test. As stated in the interviews, they expected the English studies co-ordinators to fill this gap by instructing and guiding the teachers in testing as well as in teaching. They expected that the co-ordinators would apply their pedagogical knowledge to achieve this goal by using the test format as the main form of guidance.

Conclusions

The EFL test clearly triggered a tremendous impact on classroom activities, time allotment, content and methodology. Ample new commercial teaching material – including video cassettes, TV series, cue-cards and a series of audio items – was published and marketed, designed specifically for the test. Teachers claimed to focus their teaching exclusively on the oral skills of the examination, stating: 'Of course I teach the tasks for the exam, there is no alternative but to teach as dictated by the exam'. Yet, teachers in the lower levels, whose students were not subject to the test, were more creative in their teaching, using a variety of different oral tasks. Most teachers in the upper grades also reported high anxiety, fear and pressure to cover the material, as they felt that their students' success or failure was a reflection on them. While teachers were very critical of the quality of the test, they still appreciated the status attached to it: 'The test gives oral proficiency an official status' and would not want the Ministry to cancel it.

It should be noted that no changes in the curriculum, teaching training or teaching content were introduced. The test was expected to fulfil all these roles as it became the *de facto* new curriculum, *de facto* new model of teaching methods and *de facto* new teaching material, which were very different from what was stated in the official curriculum. Thus, the test then provided the education authorities with a low-cost device that required no investment in any other educational components, as the test had the power to trigger and impose a new *de facto* policy and practice.

For the English Inspectorate, the reactions to the test (without their ever examining its real impact) were overwhelming: 'The introduction of the oral test was a great success and created a very positive educational impact, as emphasis on oral skills has been achieved not only in the higher grades but also in the lower grades.' It gave the Inspectorate much hope about the future of EFL in years to come:

We are confident that the changes in the test will result in allowing pupils to become more involved with the English language, more confident in their abilities to read and write, and above all, will enable pupils to learn English instead of learning for the Matriculation exam.

(Steiner, 1995: 15)

It should be noted that, in all of the above cases, the purposes of introducing the tests were not to measure language. In none of the tests was any attention given to the results in terms of language proficiency. In none of the cases, were students or teachers given any feedback or diagnosis that could have had input into language performance. Rather, the EFL tests were used as triggers and vehicles through which educational agendas could be carried out.

11

Cases of the use of tests

While Chapters 8 to 10 reported on empirical studies that examined the intentions and effects of using tests, this chapter reports a number of cases of the use of tests. Some of these cases are based on research, others largely represent reports and comments about these tests within the educational and the political domains.

Background

Using tests for enforcing policies is not unique to the educational context. Politicians, among others, have discovered that a test can be a useful tool for solving complex political issues that cannot be resolved through regular policy making. As was noted in Chapter 4, one specific feature that makes tests so attractive to policy makers is that they allow users to determine cutting scores in an arbitrary way and thus create quotas in a flexible manner.

A common use of tests is to grant permission to enter or to exit – whether it is for special classes, higher education, specialized organizations (e.g. the medical profession, teaching, airforce) or geographical boundaries of countries. The main rationale for using tests for such purposes is that effective and successful participation in the group (whether as learners or as graduates) requires the very knowledge that is being tested. While using tests for such purposes is clearly justified, it is often the case that tests are not used for the purposes of measuring knowledge but rather as a key to some bureaucratic agenda, such as gate-keeping the very people that the bureaucrats wish to exclude. The test then becomes the alibi, the legitimate tool for inclusion and exclusion.

In the cases that follow, tests were used mostly as means, by politicians for policy making, for selection and gate-keeping.

Using tests for gate-keeping

A case of using tests for selection and gate-keeping is the one that has been carried out in Australia with immigrants. Australia has a long history of using tests for political purposes against immigrants, from the well-documented use of a 'dictation test' at the beginning of the century, up to the 1960s when tests were used as central tools for restricting immigrants from entering Australia. Davies (1996) notes that the aim of all these tests was clearly racial exclusion. Used at the discretion of federal immigration officers, it originally required the correct transcription of 50 words in any European language and was later extended to any prescribed language. Hawthorne (1997) reports that 'within the period of 1902–1946, application of the test ensured that only around 125,000 members of "the alien races" were admitted to Australia'.

More recently, two additional tests proved to be efficient and practical solutions for the government of Australia, struggling with the problems of reducing the number of immigrants and solving issues related to refugees. Two language tests, the ACCESS and the STEP, were introduced for gate-keeping immigrants to Australia and for accepting and rejecting refugees already resident in Australia.

The ACCESS (Australian Assessment of Communicative English Skills) test was introduced in a context of deep recession, along with pressure for reduction of immigration intake to Australia. At the same time, evidence was emerging that the labour market is disadvantaged by immigrants who have limited English skills. Criticism arose regarding the effect of the low skills of immigrants and competence in the workplace. In addition to a requirement for English testing for specific occupations and vocations, the test should be undertaken by professionals as a precondition for migration or within Australia prior to professional registration. (See details of the test in Hawthorne, 1996, and McNamara, 1990.) Since 1992, the test became mandatory for different groups of immigrants for specific professions, for defining the number of points as part of the point system needed for immigration and for accompanying adult family members. The test was professionally developed to ensure high quality and minimum bias and was administered globally.

The STEP (Special Test of English Proficiency) is another example of using a test to support political decisions and for solving bureaucratic hardships. The circumstances of the development of the test within the complex political context are described in detail in Hawthorne (1997). They are related to the backlog of foreigners in Australia who had no specific status, and who were seeking permanent residence. The decision made by the Australian government was to administer the English proficiency test, in order to decide who was eligible for permanent residence. Despite providing candidates with information about the test, preparatory material, courses and preparation time, there was a strong reaction and fear of the dangers of failure from candidates. Protest was registered at the use of linguistic and qualifications criteria to decide asylum status; it was viewed as invalid and inhumane. The result of the test, whereby 78 per cent passed, does not diminish the fact that it is a strong case of using a language test to create policy and solve complex bureaucratic problems. This is summarized by Hawthorne (1997) as follows:

> Designed to appear as a gatekeeping device, STEP was in fact constructed to facilitate the Australian government's acceptance of a large majority of asylum seekers – imposing a judicious appearance of control over what was potentially an unmanageable, expensive and diplomatically awkward situation.
>
> (p. 253)

She criticizes such uses of tests, claiming that:

> The case of the STEP test offers a dramatic illustration of the increasing use of language testing by Australian authorities to achieve political purposes. . . . STEP (in alliance with qualifications assessment bodies) had a capacity to deliver to the Australian government a solution which was timely, cheap, and administratively simple – almost wholly on a user-pays basis. Three further benefits were inherent in the process. The federal government was able to impose control over a politically volatile situation, the Australian legal system was cleared of an unmanageably large backlog of refugee applications; and young PRC, Pakistani, Sri Lankan and other asylum seekers were transformed into a relatively educated and acculturated skilled migrant intake – commencing their legal permanent residence in Australia supported by a functional basis of English.
>
> (pp. 257–58)

She then cautions the profession for using tests for such purposes and argues that:

> Macro-political issues have a profound potential impact on test design, administration and outcomes. Whether benign in intent (like STEP) or otherwise, I believe they warrant detailed ethical consideration by applied linguists. In cases such as the above, where the measurement of language proficiency is clearly a pretext for achieving some broader political purpose, construct validation procedures, which are concerned with what a test purports to measure, may be an insufficient means of ensuring a test's ethicality.
>
> (p. 258)

Using tests to discriminate against ethnic groups

With the establishment of Latvia as an independent state in 1991, and the efforts to create a national cohesive society, its new government restricted citizenship to ethnic Latvians and anyone who had lived there before annexation. Many Russians had moved to Latvia after the Soviet Union invaded and annexed Latvia in 1940. A Latvian language test provided an efficient tool against the over 50 per cent ethnic Russians living in Latvia with no citizenship, including many who had lived their entire lives there. Russians were then required to pass strict language tests in the Latvian language, in order to apply for citizenship and to enter the workplace. However, as not very many of the Russians spoke Latvian, passing the test proved in most cases to be an impossible task, resulting in a large number of Russians leaving Latvia to reside in other places. In fact in 1996, a report showed a drastic decline in the number of Russians residing in Latvia: from 52 per cent to 35 per cent within a period of four years. While the language test may not be the only reason for the decline, it clearly contributed significantly to ethnic cleansing.

In October 1998 it was announced that Russians may be able to gain Latvian citizenship, after a referendum showed that 53 per cent of the voters favoured changing naturalization laws, thus making it easier for ethnic Russians to become Latvian citizens. However, the law would still require adult citizenship candidates to show competence in the Latvian language. Many Russian speakers who grew up in all-Russian communities inside Latvia regard this as unreasonable.

Using tests to raise educational level

In the USA President Clinton, in his State of the Union Address delivered on 4 February 1997, offered tests as the most practical solution for solving the troubled US education system. He proposed that

> to help schools meet the standards and measure their progress, we will lead an effort over the next two years to develop national tests of students' achievement in reading and math. Every state should adopt high national standards, so by 1999 every fourth grade student will be tested in reading and every eighth grader in math to make sure these standards are met.

While the test was voted down by the Republicans and its final destiny is not clear, it is more interesting to examine the rhetoric surrounding the test, as the US government was allocating large resources for development of tests for all students on an individual basis, believing that the tests will

upgrade the deteriorating US education system. As President Clinton concludes: '... when we aim high and challenge our students, they will be the
best in the world.'

Using tests to increase enrolment

It is common knowledge that enrolment in foreign language learning courses
at US universities are dropping. Yet it is also common knowledge that first-
year language courses provide the largest income to university language programmes as they have the largest enrolments of students when a language
requirement exists. Yet in recent years, with the increased emphasis on learning
foreign languages in secondary schools, there was a drop in enrolments in
higher education institutions as many students were exempted because of
their high school studies. High schools nowadays emphasize mostly communicative language and pay substantially less attention to grammar. A colleague of mine shared with me the strategies of her university in using tests
to ensure that enrolment is high. Her department developed tests that assess
only grammar, knowing *a priori* that this is a weak area among students. This
clearly results in students failing those tests, leading to a decision that they
will have to enrol in the required language classes.

Similar patterns were observed in bilingual classes, where tests are used to
enforce enrolment. While the criteria for such decisions are in the hands
of the tester who writes the test, the student is helpless. Upon spending a
sabbatical year in DC, I enrolled my daughter in high school in Virginia.
She was forced to enrol in the bilingual class after taking a test in English
where she did not get a perfect score. Her language proficiency is almost
'native speaker', after spending a number of years in schools in the USA and
Canada. Her 'failure' was based on a number of spelling errors, which was
enough justification to force her, against her will, to enrol in a bilingual class.

In these situations the authority is solely in the hands of the tester, who
determines the content of the test as well as the criteria for success, while
the test taker is helpless. When I demanded that she attended a 'regular'
class, as those spelling errors were not crucial for her academic success, I was
confronted with a series of bureaucratic complexities. It was only when I
threatened to take legal steps that she was allowed to participate in a regular
class. Her peers from the bilingual class, whose mothers may not be language
testers, did not have such privileges, yet they expressed a willingness to
leave. It is interesting to note that a test served as an easy instrument for that
purpose as it allows the tester to decide what to include on the tests without
any resentment on the part of test takers. In addition, as mentioned in
Chapter 3, it allows flexible cutting scores so that a programme can control,
in a very arbitrary manner, the number of test takers that pass the test. After

all, there is no supervision of what to include in a test and the tester is free to determine the content as well as the criteria and arrive at whatever decision he or she desires. Clearly the test taker is powerless and helpless – that person is in the hands of the tester and has to comply with these rules.

Thus, in these two cases, the test was used for financial reasons – to ensure that the language classes and the bilingual classes had enough students enrolled, as the number of students was directly related to the allocated funds.

Using tests to threaten

Figure 11.1 was taken from *The New York Times*, 4 September 1998. It shows how a test was used to enable the superintendent to control educational levels; he is not interested in the reasons why schools failed, nor does he specify what will be done to cure the situation in terms of funding, teacher training, etc. Rather the test serves as the only criteria for the success of the schools and for the superintendent to establish his authority. Note also that he warned them about improvement of the school's scores with no mention of the school's quality. Thus, the test serves the principal as a method of control and authority and as justification for sanctions.

---

30 Principals Receive Test-Scores Ultimatum
Los Angeles, Sept. 3 (AP) –

The head of the nation's second-largest school district has warned 30 principals that they must improve their school's test scores or lose their authority.

The superintendent of the Los Angeles Unified School District, Ruben Zacarias said that if there was no improvement by the end of the school year, he would step in to run the schools himself.

Mr. Zacarias said on Wednesday that he had sent the ultimatum because the schools failed to improve since being ranked among the 100 worst in the district last year.

He stopped short of saying the principals would be dismissed, but did say the schools would face 'personnel changes' if they did not improve performance.

Figure 11.1

Using tests to control knowledge and entrance

In this case, a state-wide test was introduced by the state of Massachusetts to certify teachers. While it can be assumed that teacher education institutions have given thought to the knowledge that prospective teachers should have, i.e. who is qualified to teach, this judgement was challenged when the state of Massachusetts decided that it would like to define that knowledge and determine who is qualified to teach by introducing a certification test. The battle as to what constitutes the appropriate knowledge for teaching was compounded by a political battle over using tests to demonstrate action and as a tool for the coming election. The definition of what constitutes knowledge was therefore determined by politics and policy makers and was battled through the cutting scores.

The test taker was clearly the victim over whom these battles were fought. In that respect it is a very good example not only of how state-wide tests served bureaucratic agendas but also of how scores can be manipulated and become tools for power and control.

On 1 July 1998, it was reported in the *New York Times* that the Massachusetts Board of Education voted to raise the passing grade for teacher certification exams and thereby failed nearly 60 per cent of the prospective teachers who took the state's first such test.

> The state prides itself on its intellectual riches and boasts that it has the highest number of colleges and universities per capita in the country. Moreover, Massachusetts is in the midst of a lively campaign for governor in which educational reform already figures as a prominent issue. So when word came in mid-June that only about 40 per cent of the nearly 1,800 test-takers had scored about the equivalent of a D on the eight-hour exam, the disturbing scores promoted a finger-pointing test at targets from the State House to the colleges that train would-be teachers.
>
> The situation became even more charged when Frank W. Haydu 3rd, the state's interim commissioner of education, proposed that a lower standard be applied to allow 56 per cent rather than 41 per cent to pass, and the State Board of Education went along, citing in part the desire to avoid lawsuits from disappointed test-takers. . . . Last Friday, Governor Celluci struck back. He announced that he would ask the Board of Education, whose nine members are mainly appointed by the governor's office, to reverse their decision and raise the passing grade back to a C, meaning an additional 263 people would flunk. And he proposed a bill that would require competency testing not only for would-be teachers but for all current ones.

It is interesting to note the different perspectives of the Governor and the commissioner of education. The Governor uses the test as a political tool; his rhetoric associates the test with political action, with high quality of education, and with determination and will. For him the existence of the test *per se* is sufficient to guarantee a high quality of education.

Every parent I talked to said, 'We want the high standards,' he said today in a telephone interview. 'As I said at the Board of Ed meeting, I started off quoting John Kennedy when he said 36 years ago: "We choose to go to the moon and do other things, not because it's easy but because it's hard." And no one ever said improving our public schools would be easy. It is hard. There will be controversy and there will be conflict and there will be stumbles, but if we stick with it, we'll get there, and the best way to get there is to hold the line on standards.'

Yet, the commissioner, who realized that his professional view did not count, refused to be used for political purposes and was forced to resign.

On Monday, Mr. Haydu, the interim education commissioner who had backed the lower standards, announced his resignation, saying he was not cut out for the campaign-season. 'I'm naïve as to what the governor's race was all about,' he said today as he left the Board of Education meeting for what he described as a long vacation.

It is worth noting that in the political and educational domain, fights are taking place on the backs of teachers who are not really part of the arguments but who are the main victims.

Fred Balboni, a would be teacher who took the test but, like all other candidates, has yet to receive his results, denounced the board vote and re-vote as 'based on swing of the political pendulum'. Balboni pointed out that in schools when a whole class does poorly on a test, the teacher assumes that there was a problem with the test itself and grades it on a curve. Others cited the critical problem that teacher candidates found out only a week before they took the test that it was not just an experiment and would actually determine whether they would be certified. And others questioned whether the test is an accurate predictor of classroom performance. In addition, some members of minorities scored worse than whites; outcomes that could also be the basis for lawsuits.

(*New York Times*, 1 July 1998)

Part

III

Uses of tests: conclusions and interpretations

This part of the book draws conclusions from the studies and cases reported in Chapters 8 to 11, leading to a model that describes the process of using tests for power and control. It then interprets the powerful uses of tests in a broader perspective, demonstrating the negative consequences of such uses of tests to education and society. It concludes by demonstrating how tests serve as symbols and ideologies.

12

Conclusions

The studies and cases on the uses of tests, as reported in Part II, demonstrate that tests were used as a means for policy making, and for power and control. In each of the studies and cases discussed in Chapters 8–11, tests were used by the authorities as instruments for carrying out, implementing and manipulating various types of policies.

In terms of intentions the tests were used to make others do what those in power believed was important, so that the tests became the vehicles through which policies and agendas were imposed. With regard to the connection between intentions and effects, it was found that in some situations such intentions materialized whereas in other situations there was a gap between intentions and effects, as specific effects occurred without there being any intentions. Thus, in the case of the reading comprehension test, there were strong effects noted, none of which being part of the intentions. The next section presents detailed conclusions from the studies and cases.

Intentions

In both the Arabic and the English tests (Chapters 9 and 10) the policy makers explicitly stated that the intentions of introducing the tests were to change the current teaching practices and to introduce new ones, while in the reading comprehension test such intentions were not explicitly stated.

In the case of the Arabic test, the national supervisor responsible for policy making stated that the reasons for introducing the test were to use it as a disciplinary tool so that it would create changes in the teaching and status of the Arabic language. By administering the test at an earlier date he had hoped that teachers would speed up the teaching of the Arabic alphabet.

Similarly, the mere fact of introducing a national test in an unpopular subject would raise its prestige and status and, consequently, would increase the motivation of teachers to teach the subject and students to learn it.

Similarly, with both versions of the English oral tests, it was explicitly stated that the intentions of introducing the tests were to make teachers and students alter their teaching and learning methods and strategies. Clearly, the policy makers perceived the test as a vehicle through which teachers would be made to teach oral language in the classrooms. In introducing the second version of the test it was even intended that the test would have an effect on the teaching of reading.

Thus, in both cases the tests were intended to be vehicles through which the central educational bodies introduced new educational goals and practices. It was publicly declared that the intentions of introducing the tests were to make all elements of the education system – teachers, students, curricula, materials and classroom practices – fall into line with the agenda of those who introduced the tests. Yet, even in situations when such intentions are not explicitly stated, as in the case of the reading comprehension test (Chapter 8), the reality was that the test had various types of effects and consequences beyond those expected. Thus, there is no guarantee that the specific intentions will occur in the direction that those who introduced the tests had hoped for.

The conclusions regarding the cases reported in Chapter 11 also showed that the intentions for introducing tests were to use them as tools for introducing and imposing policies. The tests served as a pathway for various bureaucratic agendas and to introduce policies that cannot be implemented in 'regular' ways.

This is what was behind the plan of President Clinton to introduce national tests as a method of controlling education, upgrading achievements and obtaining visibility for educational activities in the USA. While changes in policies can be achieved by taking different avenues, such as developing new curricula or investing in teacher training, the introduction of tests provides great visibility and evidence of action and is thus interpreted by the public at large as a serious approach to education.

In the case of introducing English language tests for immigrants in the Australian context, the tests were also introduced with the specific intention of using them to solve the complex bureaucratic problem of an over-abundance of immigrants. While knowledge of English was not directly related to good citizenship, an English test was used as a criterion for implementing national policy with regard to immigrants.

In the case of Latvia, the introduction of language tests in Latvian to be taken by Russian speakers was also intended to gate-keep and marginalize the Russian speakers in a society in which they were not welcome. The test thus served as a political and ideological tool and as a formal justification for discriminatory acts.

In the case of the teacher certification test in Massachusetts, the intention of using the test was to make the teaching profession appear more prestigious and elitist, as there was no real professional justification to raise or lower the cutting scores. Again, the purpose was not to use the test to improve the knowledge of teachers but rather to create an impression of a field that is selective and of higher status.

As can be learned from these studies and cases, tests are introduced in both the educational and the political contexts as tools for policy making, as they are capable of influencing and changing the behaviour of those who are affected by their scores in the direction that those who introduce them believe to be important. The tests serve as disciplinary tools, or whips, that enable those in power to enforce and carry out their policies.

Madaus (1990: 29) affirms this finding by tracing the development of the trend in the USA and its current use:

> At first results of tests were used to inform policy makers about our schools. By 1970 they had become an administrative technique to reform schools. Policy makers were shrewd enough to know they could do little to improve instruction directly – they could not mandate what goes on behind classroom doors. However, they also realized that attaching important rewards and sanctions to test scores transforms the tests into a coercive technique that can influence what is taught and learned, and how. . . . Testing is now commonly used as a bureaucratic technique for a host of high stake decisions about individuals and institutions.

Effects

Conclusions from the studies regarding the effects of introducing and using the tests showed that the tests were, in fact, capable of changing educational behaviours. Yet the nature of these effects was complex; it occurred in a number of directions and was strongly dependent on the specific context and nature of the test, as well as the specific content tested. No information is available on the effect of the cases.

In all three tests there was diversion of educational attention in areas that had not been previously explicitly taught. In the case of the Arabic test there was a change in emphasis in teaching, so that the focus was on specific vocabulary and the shortening of time devoted to the alphabet. Similarly, in the case of the English oral test, teachers started to devote more time and emphasis to oral language in the classroom. A similar pattern was found with regard to the reading comprehension test, where teaching started focusing on an area that previously had not received explicit attention. Teachers admitted that the test shifted their focus to the 'tested' topic.

Specifically, the Arabic alphabet and vocabulary had been taught before, but at a slower pace; English oral language had been taught, but with less emphasis on specific oral interactions; and reading comprehension had certainly been taught, but through other subjects. It can be concluded that through the introduction of the tests the Ministry of Education was successful in diverting the focus to new topics that it perceived as being important. By introducing a test the Ministry could guarantee the goals that would be practised for and worked towards by teachers and students in every classroom. Further, in all three cases teachers and students found the tests to be helpful in clarifying goals for teaching and learning so that the test became the object through which the authorities communicated to the education system the specific educational priorities.

In terms of the nature of the effect, the findings showed that in all three cases the teaching and learning became 'test-like', as was demonstrated in the teaching methods and in the teaching materials. As was reported with regard to the introduction of the Arabic test, the testing material and methods were an integral part of 'normal' teaching. Once the test was introduced, teaching activities became test-like, as did the new textbooks which were strongly influenced by the content of the test. In the case of the English oral test, the teaching of oral language in the classroom became test-like as well, in that it involved specific activities and formats which were identical to those included in the test. In fact the textbooks and other materials of all the three cases consisted of identical activities to those included in the tests.

Yet, it was also found that the effects of tests are often more far reaching, as they tend to be used for purposes beyond those that had originally been intended or envisioned by those who introduced them. Such was the case with the results of the reading comprehension test which it was found were used to frighten, deter, blame, punish, standardize, classify and categorize. The principals of the schools whose students took the test used the scores to judge, punish and reward. All these effects occurred regardless of the intentions of those who introduced the test and of those who had hoped that the test would be an unobtrusive measure that would lead to no side effects on the system.

Patterns of effects

It is important to note the different patterns of effects that occurred in the three studies. Based on the public statements made by those who introduced the reading comprehension test, there was no evidence that it was introduced as a disciplinary tool. Yet, it had strong disciplinary effects, with teachers and students changing their behaviours as they perceived and interpreted the test as a disciplinary tool. In the Arabic test the rationale for introducing the test was in fact to change the behaviour of teachers and learners, yet, this intended effect occurred in very limited ways. In the English test the rationale was to change the behaviour of teachers. These intentions materialized in a significantly stronger way than the decision makers had expected.

The comparison of the long-term effects of the English and the Arabic tests was revealing in that different patterns of washback emerged. The impact of the Arabic test decreased over the years to the point where it had no effect: no special teaching activities were introduced in preparation for the test, no special time was allotted, no teaching materials had been developed and awareness of the test was minimal. Thus, the teaching of the Arabic language maintained its low prestige and low status. Moreover, negative attitudes were expressed towards the test by teachers and students and the test was viewed as unimportant and of poor quality. Yet, some teachers believed that the test should continue to be administered as it did support learning.

Although unsubstantiated, some students believed that it had a potential impact on their future success. The bureaucrats, on the other hand, expressed satisfaction with the content and effect of the test and wanted to continue its administration as they feared that without the test the proficiency level, rate of progress, number of students and the prestige of Arabic would drop significantly. They therefore inserted minor changes every few years in order to create the expected washback effects.

The relatively slight modifications in the English test created a completely different effect and resulted in a significant increase of test washback. Numerous oral teaching activities in the classroom were introduced, time allotment had increased, much new courseware had been generated, a high awareness of the test was evident, and the status of the subject matter or the school had increased significantly. Although negative attitudes were expressed by teachers concerning the quality of the test, most teachers would like the test to continue. They claimed that otherwise oral proficiency would not be taught and practised and teaching would be diverted to other skills. Students expressed high anxiety and believed that the results of the test would have an effect on their success in future studies. The bureaucrats believed that the test had a very positive educational impact and a tremendous positive washback effect. They believed that adding the components of reading in the oral test also had the effect of focusing attention on that skill.

In each of the two tests the impact found in the first phase of the study differed from the impact found in the second phase. In fact, different types of long-range impact were identified; while the washback effect of the Arabic test has significantly decreased over the years, the impact of the English test has increased. It is therefore evident that washback can change over time and that the impact of tests is not necessarily stable.

It seems therefore that the effects of language tests are complex and depend on a number of factors. The next section analyses the factors that contribute to the nature of the effect of tests.

Factors contributing to effects

Low vs high stake

An important factor that can explain the effects of tests is whether the decisions that are made based on them have significance for the test taker. In the terms used in Chapter 3 – whether the results of the test lead to detrimental effects for the test takers – tests that lead to important decisions are termed high-stake tests, while low-stake tests do not have important consequences. High-stake tests lead to stronger effects. One explanation for the low effects of the Arabic test is that it was a low-stake test, in the sense that results were not used for decision making or for placement purposes. During the first year of the administration of the Arabic test, the teachers were threatened that it would lead to certain sanctions. For example, they feared being dismissed if their students did not reach a satisfactory level on the test. Yet, once the test had been in use for a few years and teachers had realized that the results had no personal or immediate impact on them, they treated it indifferently and it became a low-stake test.

The English test, on the other hand, is an example of a high-stake test as its results could have affected graduation from high school or entrance to tertiary institutions and possibly had other future consequences. That may be one reason why the test had strong effects as minor changes in the test created strong effects in terms of anxiety, production of ample new material and washback in the form of teaching and learning behaviour in the classrooms.

Language status

One significant factor that may explain the effects of language tests is the status of the language being tested, in the context in which the test is being used. The higher the status of the language, the stronger its effect will be. The differences that existed between the English and the Arabic tests, in terms of their status in the specific society where they were used, may help to explain why the first test had a stronger effect than the latter. Specifically, the Arabic language in that context had low linguistic capital value; it was a marker of the lower strata as it is spoken by groups of low status. The command of the Arabic language, therefore, has no beneficial effects on employment possibilities, academic achievement or social status (Kraemer, 1993; Ben-Rafael and Brosh, 1991).

On the other hand, the English language is highly respected in that society. It constitutes *the* valued linguistic resource after the national language and for a certain proportion of the population has even higher value than the national language. It holds the upper position in the market of languages; it is considered a power asset and a boundary marker, the importance of which can be measured by the efforts that society invests in its acquisition. Furthermore, it is gaining increasing importance in the society and is perceived by the overall population as gaining socio-economic status (Ben-Rafael, 1994; Shohamy and Donitsa-Schmidt, 1998). The effect of the test is therefore expected to be higher, given the status of English in the global linguistic market.

The purpose of the test

The different purposes of the two tests might also explain the differential effects. The Arabic test is a survey test with no consequences for individual students, yet it can have effects on teachers and schools. The English oral test is an achievement–proficiency test that is administered on an individual basis with direct consequences, often detrimental, for individuals.

The format of the test

The format of the test can also have an effect on anxiety levels and, consequently, on its impact. The Arabic test is a written test administered simultaneously to all students in the country. The English oral test, on the other hand, is administered individually in a face-to-face situation which may increase anxiety levels and consequently its impact.

The skills tested

The Arabic test measures several language skills – reading, listening and writing – while the English test measures only oral language. It may very well be that test takers have higher confidence in a multi-skilled test as they feel that they can be compensated for low proficiency in one skill by high proficiency in another.

Conclusions

The conclusions reported in this chapter have shown that when tests were used to make policy and introduce agendas by those in authority, the patterns of effects were complex. At times, intentions for impact actually occurred, while in others the effects went far beyond the intentions, indicating that tests were not isolated events and their effects could not be controlled. It was also shown that the phenomena of effects were complex, as they were dependent on various factors such as the nature, purpose, and other characteristics of the test and these could change over time. Further understanding of these factors may help to predict the form or shape of effects of different types of test. The next chapter will try to understand the main consequences of such uses of tests.

13

Process of exercising power

The conclusions of the studies and cases specifically showed that tests were introduced as disciplinary tools for policy making and for imposing the various agendas of those in authority. It was also demonstrated that such intentions did in fact materialize, as the introduction of tests led to changes in the behaviour of those who were subject to the tests. Yet, these types of effect were not easy to predict as the patterns were complex and strongly dependent on various factors. This chapter will attempt to synthesize the previous chapters by proposing a scheme that depicts the process by which the power of tests is exercised.

The components

The process of exercising power consists of two main components:

(a) *The detrimental force of tests*

This component refers to the detrimental effects of tests, as described in Chapter 3, when tests are high stake so that decisions based on their results have significant effects for the individuals being tested and for others who are affected by their results, such as parents, teachers and principals. As was shown in the previous chapters, not all effects are equally detrimental as the effects depend on the type of test, the type of test taker and the purpose and uses of the test.

(b) *The features of power of tests*

This component refers to the specific features of power of tests, as described in Chapter 4. The features of power include the administration of tests by powerful institutions, the use of the languages of science and numbers, the use of written formats, the reliance on documentation, and the employment of the objective formats.

Tests causing changes in behaviour

It is claimed here that the two components above have the power to cause a change in behaviour. The power of tests, therefore, originates in their ability to cause a change in behaviour of those who are affected by them. This change in behaviour occurs in the following way. The detrimental effect of tests, along with their powerful features, can bring a change in behaviour on the part of the test takers as those who are affected by the test will comply with the demands of the tests, given their effects. Specifically, it is argued that the detrimental effects of tests cause those who are affected by them to take certain actions in order to maximize their scores. They can gain the benefits associated with success on the test or avoid the consequences associated with failure of it by changing their behaviours in line with the demands of the tests. In other words, it is the motivation to succeed on tests, especially on high-stake tests, that causes a change in the behaviour of test takers as they are willing to do almost anything to succeed, being aware of the benefits associated with high scores (or the punishments associated with low scores). It should be noted that behavioural changes occur not only in test takers but also in others who are indirectly affected by the results of tests. Thus, teachers may change their teaching strategies as the success of their students is often viewed as a reflection of their teaching, and parents may invest in private tutoring for their children as success on tests may be perceived as a reflection of their parenting.

Many examples that illustrate changes in behaviour caused by the power of tests were included in the studies presented in Chapters 8 to 10, where teachers changed their teaching and learning strategies in order to gain higher scores. In one of the examples presented in Chapter 2 (p. 9), a principal resorted to the unethical behaviour of denying some students the right to be tested, for fear that their low scores would hurt the school's average score, leading to detrimental effects on his school. In another example in Chapter 2, a teacher changed the path of teaching to topics known to be included on an impending test.

It is thus the detrimental force of tests, along with their features of power, that are capable of *causing* those who are affected by the results of tests to change their behaviour and comply with the demands of the tests in order to maximize their scores and gain the benefits associated with high scores. Thus, the power and authority of tests originates from their capability of causing a change in behaviour among those who are affected by them.

This relationship is similar to relationships observed in economic models where producers and consumers will take steps to maximize their profits. Consumers in such situations are willing to behave differently in order to gain profits. The process is in line with the model introduced by Bourdieu (1991) entitled 'the economy of practice'. Bourdieu argues that various commodities which may not be governed by strictly economic logic (e.g. may not be oriented towards financial gain) may none the less concur with a logic that is economic in a broader sense, insofar as they are oriented towards the augmentation of *some* kind of 'capital' (e.g. cultural or symbolic capital) or the maximization of *some* kind of symbolic 'profit' (e.g. honour or prestige). In testing situations, test takers may wish to maximize their scores, which can be translated into better jobs or certificates of entrance, or economic gains such as increased salaries, better jobs and expansion of economic opportunities. Yet, high scores are also translated into gains in terms of recognition by teachers, parents and peers, or getting the prestige and honour of being the best in the group, even if it does not bring immediate financial profit. Thus, maximizing scores on tests obeys an economic logic, and models of maximizing benefits in the broad sense of obtaining symbolic capital and profits, without being economic in the narrow sense of purely financial and material gains.

Exercising power and control

The next step in the process of exercising the power of tests, is when tests are used as a *means* of enforcing policies by those in authority. This refers to situations when decision makers take advantage of the phenomenon of the power of tests to cause behavioural changes, as discussed earlier, in order to change the behaviours of those who are affected by the tests in line with certain agendas which they wish to introduce. This refers to situations, described in Chapters 8 to 11, when decision makers take advantage of the phenomenon of the power of tests in order to change the behaviour of those affected by the tests, in line with certain agendas.

The process is depicted in Figure 13.1. Part (A) represents the power of the test to cause a change in the behaviour of those affected by their results. Part (B) represents the phenomenon whereby tests are used by decision makers and those in authority as tools for introducing agendas and enforcing policies. Part (C) depicts the effects and impact of such policies, whereby the anticipated changes occur in very complex ways depending on a number of factors. Part (D) shows the societal and educational consequences of such uses of tests.

The following is an example of how such a process occurs. Policy makers believe that a certain language area, say reading comprehension, should be

(A) *The origin of the power of tests*
The detrimental force of tests *along* with their features of power **cause** those who are affected by the results of tests to change their behaviour and comply with the test's demands in order to maximize their scores and gain the benefits associated with high scores.

↓

(B) *Manipulations*
Being aware of the capability of tests to affect behaviours leads those in power to introduce tests as **means** of creating and imposing changes in behaviours in line with specific agendas.

↓

(C) *Effects*
Such use of tests has effects, yet the type and size of effects are complex and dependent on multiple factors such as status of the topic, purpose of the test, skill tested and whether the test is of high or low stakes.

↓

(D) *Consequences**
The consequences of such uses of tests for education and society are a greater focus on the topic, narrowness of the knowledge, unethical behaviours, re-definition of knowledge, punishment, gate-keeping and controlling of education.

* The list of consequences is based on information provided in Chapter 14.

Figure 13.1   The power of tests – origins, manipulations, effects and consequences

taught. This decision is often a reaction to public or media demands, a conference an inspector had attended, or a wish to demonstrate control and action. A test is then introduced and individuals are forced to participate. Hence, the test becomes a means by which the policy makers communicate priorities to the system. In a high-stake situation (i.e. when the results of the test are used for important decisions about individuals or programmes) teachers react by teaching the topic. They experience fear and anxiety as students, principals and parents demand preparation for this high-stake test. Since teachers have no explicit knowledge of how to teach the topic they turn to the most immediate pedagogical source, the test itself, to learn how to carry out and comply with the new orders. The test becomes the single most influential pedagogical source, and the *de facto* knowledge. Teachers are reduced to 'following orders' – a frustrating role as their responsibility increases while their authority diminishes. The test then becomes the device through which power and control are exercised authoritatively, legitimizing the power of bureaucrats and other élite groups. This seems to be an unethical way of policy making, yet usually carries no resentment whatsoever on the part of those who are affected by it.

As will be shown, most tests are introduced without involving teachers. Yet, excluding teachers – those who are responsible for delivering the instructional information – is an unethical and a humiliating act based on the view that the role of teachers is to carry out orders, not to initiate, create, or contribute.

14

Consequences

In the previous chapters the uses of tests were described, their intentions and effects analysed and a scheme for describing the process of exercising control was proposed. This chapter will move beyond the immediate effects of the specific tests and cases, and towards understanding the consequences of tests in a broader context of use. It will argue that such uses of tests for power and control have negative consequences for education and society.

Narrowing the knowledge

Arguments against using standards and testing as the engine of reform (Koretz, Madaus, Haertal and Veaton, 1992) have been documented repeatedly (House, 1998). They consistently show how similar attempts have failed in the past, that instruction narrows and that test scores are artificially inflated to the point of questionable validity, by teaching to the tests.

As early as 1877, Latham (quoted in Spolsky, 1995, 1998) characterized examination

> . . . as an 'encroaching power' that was influencing education, blurring distinctions between liberal and technical education, narrowing the range of learning through forcing students to prepare by studying with crammers and cramming schools. Teaching in England was becoming subordinate to examinations rather than its master.
>
> (1998: p. 2)

House claimed that the notion of collecting data in the belief that it would 'drive education improvement' is common yet very questionable. Such thinking seems far removed from how learning functions. It is similar to measuring the temperature as a cure for an illness.

The rationale behind such an agenda is generally that teachers and students are not trying hard enough, and that students are not sufficiently motivated to achieve in school. If one puts pressure on them through threats or failures, teachers and students would try harder and achieve more. Yet many students cannot attain these standards, even after extra years of instruction in special classes – in fact, a certain percentage of the population will never attain the prescribed standard. From the studies reported here it is evident that the introduction of tests produced mostly 'test language'.

Turning tests into a means for change, into instrumental devices for promoting agendas, narrows the process of education. While the introduction of a test can be influential in terms of changing the focus and increasing awareness, the educational effectiveness of tests introduced in such ways cannot be very high, because the approach narrows the process of education, making it merely instrumental and not meaningful.

Freedman (1993), in studying the effect of writing tests, demonstrates how high-stake tests undermined students' work and attitudes in both obvious and subtle ways and did not lead to improved instruction. In a study comparing the US and British writing classes, she found that in Britain, where examinations were part of the system, the classes had to adhere to requirements that inhibited the teachers' abilities to build a coherent curriculum. They also restricted the amount and kind of writing the students did and, in effect, the pressure of the examinations took over. Students who were not taking part in the examinations were motivated by their own decision making and by being part of a community working together, but when writing for the examination, however, this rarely happened. These issues were even more problematic for teaching bilingual writers, who may have learned from specific corrections and by having a series of errors pointed out in detail. The conclusions reached by the US teachers was that any kind of high-stake examination with associated curriculums would harm their students' writing development. She claimed therefore that 'a system of high-stake examinations – even well-designed performance-based examinations – provides a flawed foundation on which to build a national educational reform movement. In fact, examinations have the potential to move away from, rather than toward, the point we all want to reach' (Freedman, 1993: 26). Testing should follow, not lead, a reform effort. With regard to the area of writing, she claimed that when national examinations took control of something as personal as writing, a distant examiner, rather than the teacher and students, ended up owning the writing. Moreover when the examination was high stake, as when it had an effect on students' future life and career, it put formidable pressures on the classroom and was particularly likely to have negative effects on the curriculum.

It is important to note that these observations were not limited to objective type tests. As was noted in Chapter 3, even tests which were based on open items or performance type tasks eventually turned to narrowing the learning, as tests turn them into narrow objective statements. The example of the writing tests described by Freedman (1993) shows how large-scale direct writing tests move away from the nature of the trait and towards an objective nature constrained and controlled by time, content, topic, scoring rubrics and raters who are not allowed to deviate from the assigned truth.

Thus, when reforms were introduced through tests, the tests were no more than a quick fix that overlooked the need to attain meaningful comprehension and a deep insight into a topic, especially with regard to an external test that could represent no more than a limited body of knowledge on any subject. She concludes that '. . . the path to curriculum reform through examinations, though tempting, remains elusive' (p. 29).

The studies reported in Chapters 8 to 10 demonstrated how the quality of the knowledge created as a result of the test could be defined mostly as 'test language'. It was shown that the intention of creating changes in the teaching of English and Arabic by introducing tests, could not ensure meaningful changes in pedagogy; in fact, these pedagogical changes rarely took place. Further, introducing changes through tests did not mean that testers made resources available to carry out such changes. Often decision makers relied exclusively on the tests to create the changes without guaranteeing the basic resources such as smaller class sizes, reduced workloads for teachers and the training needed to carry out such tasks. It is clear that pressure and sanctions alone are not enough.

Met (pers. comm.) observed similar patterns with regards to the introduction of state-wide tests:

> Originally envisioned as performance assessment tied to forward looking learning goals in each of four disciplines, feasibility constraints associated with costs, psychmometric issues, and quick turn around times (critical for students' for graduation) will require close ended, multiple choice tests. These tests, in turn, are likely to result in impoverished curriculum and instruction. Teachers teach to the test and reduce the curriculum to that which is tested, despite successful efforts over the last decade to improve instruction through constructivism and related performance-based approaches to teaching.

In the studies reported in Chapters 8 to 10, it became evident that the tests which were used instrumentally resulted in no more than a quick fix. There was no serious discussion with any of the tests of what the topic tested meant; rather the tests were introduced as therapies for solving problems. In the case of the reading comprehension test, schools added reading comprehension hours at the expense of subject areas such as geography and history, rather than integrating reading comprehension into the subject areas. This represents a simplistic and instrumental solution. Similarly, with regard to the Arabic test, it was shown how the complex problem of teaching Arabic was reduced to specific and defined components such as the teaching of the alphabet and some vocabulary items. This provided evidence that those who introduce the tests are more interested in simplistic solutions, where gains can be seen immediately, than in meaningful changes.

Such uses of tests re-created the contents in testing terms – test-like material, test-like teaching – and narrowed the scope of the topic being taught. The knowledge created through the tests is often referred to as 'institution-alized knowledge'; its main characteristics are that it is narrow, simplistic and often in contradiction to expert knowledge. After all, the information included on tests is only a representation of real knowledge; it is monological, based on one instrument (a test), on one occasion, detached from meaning-ful context and usually with no feedback for improvement.

Using tests as the *de facto* knowledge provides only 'a quick fix', an instant solution that overlooks the complexities of subject matter and is not mean-ingful for improvement. Weiss (1977) differentiates between the *instrumental* impact of tests, characterized as short range and goal oriented, and the *conceptual* impact, which is long range and meaningful, followed by discus-sions on the nature of the trait, methods of teaching, and agreed upon criteria of quality. In none of the tests reported above was there any serious discussion with teachers or students about the tested topics, whether they were learnable or measurable. For bureaucrats, these simplistic and instant solutions are very attractive as they offer instant evidence of impact in their usually short terms in office. As Freire (1985: 23–4) states:

> The more bureaucratic the evaluators are, not just from an administrative point of view but above all from an intellectual view, the narrower and more inspection like the evaluation will be.

Madaus (1990: 30) therefore argues that:

> Testing has become a defining technology, it promotes certain values and diminishes others; it is a way for people to explain themselves and others; it is the way we describe or point at what's important for our schools to attain; and it is even used to describe our relative educational standing in the world.

Redefining *de facto* knowledge contradicting existing knowledge

The negative consequences of using tests in such ways are that tests are capable of redefining knowledge and that this 'new' knowledge contradicts existing knowledge as defined by the curriculum. It is the power of tests that is considered as the *de facto* new knowledge. Yet, in most societies the redefinition of knowledge through tests creates two parallel systems: one manifested through the curriculum or policy documents, the other reflecting bureaucratic aspirations through tests. These two systems often directly contradict one another, and there are many examples which demonstrate this phenomenon. Consider the case of a country that declares a multilingual policy, yet only one language, say English, is tested. In another country there are two official languages, yet only the powerful language is tested. Marisi's (1994) work shows that those speaking Quebec French are not considered native speakers by the ACTFL testing guidelines.

Bernstein (1986) refers to the two systems as primary and secondary; primary is talk, while secondary is practice – *de facto* and more relevant since it has the enforcing power. There is therefore an 'official' story and a 'real' story, which is exercised by tests and pushed by bureaucrats, and is often not known to the public. It is clearly the testing policy which is the *de facto* policy as 'tests become targets for contending parties who seek to maintain or establish a particular vision of what education and society should be' (Noah and Eckstein, 1992: 14).

Creating new power forces is even more obvious with regard to language tests. The power of tests has reached such high levels that it is now a common belief that what is tested is important. Simply the fact that something is being tested, creates a belief that it had reached status and importance. Tests have become the main indicators of status.

This is especially a widespread phenomenon in situations where testing is compulsory – whether as part of matriculation examinations or as entrance to a country. In countries that have 'end of secondary school' subjects that are not included in national examinations, much effort is exerted in demanding that they should be included – for example, foreign language educators would very much like to see foreign languages included in the NAEP examinations in the USA. Ormsby (1998) reports that speakers of indigenous groups view it as offensive that their languages are not included in end of high school tests. They clearly view the policy failing to give importance to these languages. They lobby strongly for including these languages in national tests, believing that it will grant the languages higher status in the country.

The negative consequences of this phenomenon are clear: it is not the subject that is important, but how certain groups and policy makers view it; it is an ideological and artifical way of upgrading and prioritizing education; and the power lies with the tests and those who decide to use them to grant authority to certain subjects.

There is no doubt that one of the main reasons why the test of English, reported in Chapter 10, was so influential was because of the power of the

English language. The test, in the case of the English language and its role in the world today, served as an amplifying device to perpetuate its power and to inflate the power of English even further.

It is also interesting to note how tests help to upgrade certain languages and downgrade others. Many countries will include tests of English on final high school examinations and as entrance examinations to higher education, but they will not include tests of other languages. Thus, testing specific languages grants them more power than they already have; conversely, not testing certain languages reduces their power even further. Clearly, the decision as to which languages will be tested is often left to bureaucrats and other policy makers who have the authority to grant power to what they view as important. In many countries the imposition of the English test at the end of secondary education remains unchallenged and, therefore, guarantees the continuous domination of the language in the school system – and often in society as well.

The following is an example of exercising control though tests in the area of redefining knowledge. There is an untaught topic or area that the educational leadership believes should be taught and mastered. This decision is often a reaction to public or media demands for action. To ensure that the new topic is taught, a test is introduced because this is the easiest and quickest way for policy makers to demonstrate action and authority and to guarantee a change in behaviour. If the test is high stake it serves as an efficient tool for changing the behaviours of teachers and students. Since teachers experience fear and anxiety as students, principals, and parents all demand preparation of this high-stake test, they change their behaviour and start teaching for the test, as the test serves as a model of knowledge and as an immediate pedagogical source. (In situations when there is no information about the content of the test, rumours about the test serve a similar role.) Over the years, new books are written and workshops are designed to prepare teachers for the test. Thus, if no meaningful professional teacher training takes place, the test becomes the *de facto* curriculum. Even when a curriculum does exist, it becomes subordinate to the test. In centralized 'authoritative' education systems, tests become the major devices through which the leadership communicates educational priorities to teachers and through which they introduce their agendas. While the introduction of a test can be influential in terms of changing the focus of teaching, it is not known what the impact would have been if the Ministry of Education had decided to change teaching practices through other means, such as workshops, in-service courses, or new textbooks.

It is interesting to note that this pattern of communicating agendas through tests is then applied in the classroom as well. A similar pattern emerges when teachers receive the message from the education authorities that tests are to be used to effect a change of behaviour; they tend to use this method with their own students in the classroom by using more tests.

Unethical and undemocratic ways of making policy

Using tests to create *de facto* policies can be viewed as an undemocratic and unethical procedure as it represents those in power, and is often neither declared publicly nor discussed openly with the subjects of the tests. It is dictated from above without including those who are affected by the tests – teachers and test takers.

Implementing policy in such ways is based on threats, fear, myths and power, by convincing people that without tests learning will not occur. It is an unethical way of making policy; it is inappropriate to force individuals in a democratic society. Thus, tests are used to manipulate and control education and become the devices through which educational priorities are communicated to principals, teachers and students. In the reading comprehension test it was clear that, by applying the categories of Foucault (1979), the uses of tests led to unethical behaviour: the tests were used to quantify, observe, normalize, standardize, classify, punish, judge, and for surveillance.

Using tests to make policy and shape education systems is not ethical since the test taker does not really benefit from such testing. If most tests do not provide a test taker with diagnostic information about his or her performance, there are no clear benefits for the test taker. In fact in these situations it is the test taker who is paying the price for the benefits gained by the authorities in power. Thus, test takers are being used as they become the instruments through which bureaucratic manipulations are performed. The test taker pays the price as he or she goes through pressure, tension, change in behaviour, anxiety and some of the other negative experiences which were voiced in Chapter 2. For test takers who cannot succeed on tests the consistent negative feedback can be damaging.

> It is a pretty battering experience for a kid who might be having difficulty with a subject – or who might be creative, or who might think differently – to constantly get back the message that you are not good enough. Most of these tests are not going to make you think in ways that, as adults, you might think of as important.
>
> (Peter Cookson, quoted in Steinberg, 1999: 18)

Therefore, another unethical dimension of tests is when they are used for power and control and for making policies. Not providing meaningful information to students can be viewed as avoiding responsibility for the effect of the examination on learning. It can be considered an unjust use of the information, as it is used for different purposes than those known to the test taker.

If tests are meant to assess knowledge, this certainly was not obviously in all the cases reported in this book. Tests were used for other purposes, for serving diverse political and bureaucratic agendas in different contexts and levels. Policy makers used tests to manipulate educational systems, to control curricula, to create new knowledge, and to impose new textbooks and teaching methods. Bureaucrats use tests to define and standardize language knowledge, to raise proficiency, to communicate educational agendas, to give an illusion of action and to act as an excuse for no action. At the school level, principals use school-wide examinations to drive teachers to teach and use tests and quizzes to motivate students to learn and to impose discipline. On the political level, tests are used to create *de facto* language policies, to raise the status of some languages and to lower those of others, to control citizenship, to include or exclude, to gate-keep, to maintain power of the élite, to offer simplistic solutions to complex problems and to raise the power of nations to be 'the best in the world'.

Conclusions

This chapter demonstrated the negative consequences on society and education of using tests as a method of power and control. It showed how such use of tests does not lead to improved learning or to higher achievement, but creates parallel systems in which tests become the *de facto* knowledge – often in contradiction to more sophisticated systems – and is an artificial way of granting power. It was also claimed that such uses of tests are in fact an unethical and undemocratic way of making policies.

15

Symbols and ideologies

Tests, it was demonstrated, are powerful instruments; they are being used by those in authority to manipulate educational systems to suit the agendas of those who hold power. Such use of tests, it was argued, has negative consequences for learning and is unethical and undemocratic. Yet, the dominance of tests is unchallenged, unmonitored and uncontrolled, and they have enormous trust and support on the part of the public and institutions. Tollefson (1995) identifies three aspects of power: state, discourse and ideology; tests represent all three. State power, in terms of bureaucrats; discourse power, as tests are imposed by unequal individuals (the tester and the test taker); and ideological power, i.e. belief of what is right and what is wrong, what is good knowledge and what is not, what is worthwhile economically and what is not. The ease with which tests have become so accepted and admired by all those who are affected by them is remarkable. How can tests persist in being so powerful, so influential, so domineering and play such enormous roles in our society?

One answer to this question is that tests have become symbols of power for both individuals and society. Based on Bourdieu's (1991) notion of symbolic power, this chapter will examine the symbolic power and ideology of tests and the specific mechanisms that society invented to enhance such symbolic power.

Symbolic power

Symbolic power, according to Bourdieu (1991: 192), is:

> a power which the person submitting to grants to the person who exercises it, a credit with which he credits him, a fides, an auctoritas, with which he entrusts him by placing his trust in him. It is a power which exists because

the person who submits to it believes that it exists. . . . the politician derives his political power from the trust that a group places in him. He derives his truly magical power over the group from faith in the representation that he gives to the groups and which is a representation of the group itself and of its relation to other groups. As a representative linked to those he represents by a sort of rational contract (the programme), he is also a champion, united by a magical relation of identification with those who, as the saying goes, 'pin all their hopes on him'.

The power of those who introduce tests derives from the trust that those who are affected by the tests place in them. This, according to Bourdieu, is some type of a rational contract between those in power who want to dominate and those who want to be dominated and grant those in power the authority to do so. Thus, as much as those in power want to control and dominate, there is also a strong willingness on the part of the subjects to be dominated and controlled so as to perpetuate their existing social structure.

The willingness to be dominated originates from the fact that tests, or other powerful instruments (e.g. money, status), are capable of perpetuating and maintaining existing powers. Tests, then, are instrumental in affirming societal powers and roles and hence maintain social order. According to Bourdieu, there is an unwritten agreement, a contract, between those in authority who introduce tests and those whose worth is being assessed by tests, as tests serve as a power symbol for both groups and as a vehicle for maintaining social order. Tests, then, have become acceptable and recognized as they serve useful roles for those tested, providing them with constant recognition of how good they are. Tests are a recognized political institution that serves the cause of those with vested interests, thus their symbolic domination. For bureaucrats, administrators and élite groups, tests symbolize social order. For parents, who often do not trust schools and teachers, tests provide an indication and a symbol of control, and for various élite groups tests provide a means for perpetuating dominance.

Mechanism for enhancing symbolic power

A number of strategies are used to enhance and cultivate such symbolic power; these mechanism are accepted by both the dominators and dominated, all in an effort to perpetuate and guarantee their continued status and roles in society.

An unwritten contract among those with vested interests

This mechanism is based on the notion that the symbolic power of tests is derived and enhanced by the fact that a number of groups co-operate with one another to maintain social order and to perpetuate existing knowledge.

This unwritten agreement is often a conspiracy of silence. The most obvious example is the acceptance of problematic test scores by bureaucrats to arrive at policy decisions, whether it is in issues of acceptance of immigrants, providing citizenship or granting certificates of entrance. Schwandt (1989: 12) observes how data, produced by testers, are used in the hands of bureaucrats:

> As masters of the tools of scientific analysis, these experts generate empirical evidence – scientifically based knowledge – that managers use to enhance their authority and control.

Enhancing the symbolic power is done in co-operation with power institutions such as academic institutions who will use tests as the main and often 'the' single criteria for accepting students to their institutions – thus granting them their symbolic power. Take, for example, an entrance test such as the SAT. Schwartz (1999: 51) notes:

> Why, then do American high-school students feel increasingly compelled to devote substantial time and money to the pursuit of higher S.A.T. scores? The answer lies in an unspoken but self-perpetuating alliance between college-admission officers, the College Board and test-preparation companies. While these groups sometimes have conflicting agendas, each plays a part in supporting the S.A.T.s – and attributing significance to relatively small differences in students' scores.

Clearly, if higher education institutions will decide one day not to use tests, the economic value of tests will decrease substantially.

There is also an unwritten contract between institutions and parents. Institutions are interested in using tests for authority, and parents, in return, grant them the power and authority as tests can maintain and perpetuate their own status in society. House (1998) notes that raising educational standards through testing appeals to the middle classes, partly as it allows their children to gain access to better jobs – and, for some, it is a code word for restricting minority access. Tests, then, are instrumental for both institutions and parents in justifying and reaffirming their status and continue to maintain the existing social order.

Determining 'rites of passage'

Another mechanism for enhancing the symbolic power of tests is to use them as a way of perpetuating class differences and as screening devices to excluding those whom those in power do not wish to include. In these situations tests become useful procedures for controlling entry, leading to gate-keeping and ensuring that the élite consists only of 'our' people. Schwartz (1999) notes that lower test scores by blacks are the single biggest barrier to racial equality in the USA.

The use of cutting scores, discussed in Chapters 4 and 6, provides an effective mechanism for controlling the rite of passage and creating artificial boundaries. Bourdieu (1991: 120) writes that:

> However, social magic always manages to produce discontinuity out of continuity. The paradigmatic example of this, and my starting point, is the competitive academic examination (*concours*): between the last person to pass and the first person to fail, the competitive examination creates differences of all or nothing that can last a lifetime. The former will graduate from an elite institution like the *Ecole Polytechnique* and enjoy all the associated advantages and perks, while the latter will become a nobody.

Spolsky (1998: 12) also notes:

> the sad truth [is] that most users act as though the score a student receives is a real absolute measure with an immediate non-contextualized interpretation, and as though there is a real difference between a student who scores 597 and one who scores 601.

In this way tests serve as means for creating social orders, for perpetuating class differences and for blocking the entrance of those who are not wanted.

Yet, an interesting phenomenon is that even low-status groups, minorities and immigrants who are not part of the élite, and who are constantly excluded and rejected by tests, also have an overwhelming respect for tests and often fight against their abandonment. Their behaviour is similar to that of victims believing they are unworthy, mostly as a result of the effective propaganda that turns tests from symbols to ideologies, as will be argued in the section on ideology below.

In many countries in the world today the status of English is raised while the status of national languages is lowered, as English is declared by those in power as a modern lingua franca, a passport to higher education, although only a small percentage of the population speaks it.

Another dimension in many countries is where only 'the privileged' have the right to be tested. Such privileges can be gained by attending the right school, having a graduating diploma, being born in the country where the tests are administered, etc. The most obvious example is the situation in which immigrants are not included in the testing pool. In an example in Chapter 2, it was shown how some students were not allowed to be tested as they were considered by the authorities to be 'low level students'. Yet at the same time in large-scale assessment all students are being required to be tested, which forces them into a situation where they end up being classified and eventually become subjects of the boundaries. Chapter 5 discusses how the rites of passage vary in accordance with the education systems so that, in many countries, only the privileged have the right to be tested.

Controlling and perpetuating knowledge

A widely used method for enhancing the symbolic power of tests is controlling the content and knowledge of tests. Thus, tests include only what Bourdieu refers to as the knowledge that is socially recognized as legitimate by those in power. Accordingly, those who write tests include their own knowledge and can thus ensure difficulties for those who do not 'belong', leading to their rejection from the power group. By not recognizing other forms of knowledge it is easy to limit the access of 'others' and at the same time maintain the knowledge exclusively to those who share it. This strategy is easily practised when representatives of 'the other knowledge' are not included in testing committees.

It is interesting to trace the development of this mechanism as a means for enhancing symbolic power. In the past few years the public has been concerned with the fairness of tests. The use of objective items made tests more trustworthy as they were also considered objective. Yet, the knowledge upon which these objective tests were based remained the same; it still represented those in power. In addition this knowledge was now assessed through 'scientific' procedures which the public could not even critique, as the field was in the hands of experts and specialists using terminology and statistics that were not accessible to lay people. Thus, the situation now is that élite groups continue to control knowledge and, with the aid of tests, they continue to perpetuate it. Furthermore, they now have a legitimate mechanism of control.

It is not difficult to see the connection between the content of the test and perpetuating power, as the decisions made on the basis of these tests lead to high-stake decisions such as selection, controlling immigration, accepting jobs, graduating from high schools, entering universities, obtaining high-ranking jobs or entering élite institutions.

Banks (1998) shows how tests are used to block the passage of African-American children by testing them on white culture only; no white Americans protest against it. In an example from Israel, where both Hebrew and Arabic are official languages, those in power have decided that only knowledge of Hebrew, by passing a Hebrew test, provides the right of passage to Israeli higher education institutions, thus ensuring that many Arabs are excluded. Needless to say, no Jewish test takers protest against this decision.

Yet, in the attempt to develop fairer and more objective tests, little attention was paid to the knowledge on which the tests had been based. The bodies of knowledge did not change. On one hand, tests became more democratic in terms of their techniques – based on objective items and applying scientific criteria of analyses – but, on the other hand, tests continued to represent traditional systems of selection, as the knowledge included in these tests did not differ significantly from the knowledge used in previous periods. Thus, in the same way that the knowledge a person was required to master in the past was determined by élite groups who were exposed to different education systems and the test prevented lower classes from being selected, the knowledge remained unchanged even in the era of mass testing. The only difference was that everyone had the right and the opportunity to be tested. It became clear, however, that those coming from different backgrounds, different traditions, and different education systems were not equally enabled to master the required knowledge. Thus, while the methods of selection and acceptance were changed, the substance of what the test taker was expected to know did not. That was a continuation of the situation in which those writing the tests continued to use *their own* knowledge as criteria for acceptance into the élite groups of society. The hope that the introduction of tests would democratize society did not really happen. In a way, it is a worse situation, as the élite that determines the content of the test now has a mechanism to gate-keep – objective tests, that the public trusts and can therefore be used to perpetuate the élite and its domination even more.

Creation of dependence

This mechanism refers to the fact that children are being tested from an early age. Children and parents are accustomed to estimating their worth through tests. It is not uncommon that children are being tested at the age of 3 or 4 in order to discover hidden talents, to be accepted to prestigious nursery schools, to measure IQ, to confirm developmental problems, to enter first grade or to be streamed to special education classes. The public becomes dependent and hooked on tests, developing unchallenged trust in their results and in their symbolic power. From an early age people are socialized to believe that tests are the prime indicators of their societal values. Steinberg (1999: 18) refers to a 'compulsion to test' and describes it as an 'epidemic' that is spreading from one school district to the next. He points to the fact that

> By the time they were ready to graduate from sixth grade last June, New York City fifth graders had taken eight standardized tests over the previous 14 months; this year's fourth-grade reading test, to be given statewide next week, will take three days to administer. In Chicago, pupils took 12 standardized tests from the winter of third grade through the spring of fourth-grade reading and eighth-grade math.

Such socialization to testing from an early age is what Bourdieu refers to as 'habitus', habits that children engage in from childhood. In terms of testing, it is the view that testing is crucial to success in life. It is at an early age that tests become the main authority and symbol of power, turning it into a habit, and developing a dependence on it. Tests, then become the tools of trust and a symbol of direction, guidance and social habits.

Granting test scores economic value

This mechanism is widely used for enhancing power and it refers to translating success and failure on tests into currency – economic value that estimates the worth of people. This is not always translated into currency, it may also be in the form of a certificate, promotion or other devices that can be translated or converted to some type of reward that society values. For younger test takers this often means approval or disapproval of parents, as they create pre-dispositions about the 'worth' of their children according to their test scores.

An effective mechanism for enhancing symbolic power is therefore to give the product such market value. Market value can be in forms of 'acceptance' to a prestigious programme, immigrant visa (in Australia), citizenship (in Latvia), a teaching certificate (in Massachusetts) or high school diploma. It can also be in the form of promotion, job and money. In this case testing agencies and institutions, governments and élites work together, in an unwritten contract, to support one another.

The high economic value placed in tests also explains why test takers are willing to spend big sums of money for test preparation courses and thus support a growing industry that just makes the rich even richer. In these situations the tests perpetuate power and raise the market value of the élites.

The combination of language and tests

The power of language, especially of the English language, has been argued in a number of places (Phillipson, 1992; Pennycook, 1994). Thus, the combination of two sources of power – language and tests – is a very effective mechanism for enhancing symbolic power as well. Such is the case with language tests, which bring together two very powerful institutions: language and tests, creating a new powerful institution that is even more difficult to challenge. When a language is tested in higher education institutions as criteria for acceptance, the symbolic power of the test and the language are enhanced significantly, presenting society with an extremely powerful tool. Ormsby (1998) provides an example of indigenous groups in Mexico demanding that their language also be tested so as to enhance their power. A similar reason was used in the Arabic test described in Chapter 9, where there is a belief that if the language is tested its power will be enhanced. Clearly, the symbolic power of TOEFL gains its strong value from being both the symbol of a test and of a powerful language.

Further, most institutions in the USA use tests of English as entrance criteria for higher education as well as to English classes, in the case of immigrants willing to enter mainstream classes. It is remarkable how these powerful language tests are accepted by society as the 'correct' device for screening people. Yet neither linguists nor testers really know the level of language that is needed for immigrants to function academically, either in higher education or in schools. How crucial the knowledge of language is for academic success is still an open question that does not have empirical answers. Yet, language testers determine cutting scores and thus pretend to know the correct answer and often inform those responsible for admission what score is required. Decision makers, as was noted above, are happy that testers provide them with this information, so they do not have to make the decision. It is clear, some testers claim, that this is one more example where scores can be used in almost any way, depending on the particular political agenda of the user.

Thus, it is easy to rely on language knowledge and on tests to create symbolic power. It is clear that for the language testers, symbolic power can be enhanced even further by the fact that he or she is in charge of an area believed by those in power (native speakers) to be of even greater value, given their own knowledge of the language.

Textual power

Lemke (1995) refers to the political power of the texts, arguing that language as exemplified through texts is powerful. Tests are texts, and texts have meanings – meanings which can be translated into power.

Fillmore (1981) discusses the type of texts used in tests as being very different from the typical texts that people read in non-testing situations. He describes the behaviour of the test takers with regard to these texts and genres as being subversive, whereby the test taker is making an effort to accommodate 'the truth' that is owned by the tester. An additional dimension is the powerful message delivered through the discourse of the instruction of most tests. These are written in a cold language and in a most authoritative form, dictating one type of behaviour with no deviations whatsoever. The instructions of the test imply that the test taker is dishonest, has bad intentions and is only looking for ways to circumvent good behaviour. Thus, it is through the discourse of both the texts and the instruction that the symbolic power of tests is enhanced, as both are authoritative and patronizing and reduce the test taker to a powerless creature whose role is simply to follow orders.

Ceremonial rituals

An important mechanism that enhances the symbolic power of tests is the use of a number of rituals and ceremonial features in the forms of rules and behaviours, which only take place during tests. This is what Foucault refers to as 'the ceremony of power'. For many of these rules there is no rational explanation except the need to create symbolic power. Some of the rules of tests are to have distance between test writer and test taker, to write with certain pencil numbers, in certain types of notebooks, carrying nothing more than the minimum possessions, to have a monitor in the room, not to talk to any of their peers, to ignore any misunderstandings, not to ask any questions, and to perform the task within a very rigid time constraint, no questions asked. In addition, there is secrecy and mystery surrounding the test. The use of complex statistical formulas that the public cannot understand as well as the use of sophisticated ways of using testing technology add to the symbolic power. The context of tests creates a set of rules that are different from 'normal life' so that fear, respect and authority are created by those who dictate the rules. Just how different these ceremonial features are from real life can be learned from an interview that Steinberg conducted with Joshua Halberstam, who had just written a book about test preparation. Steinberg (1999: 18) quotes Halberstam as saying:

> For kids who have never taken these tests, for young kids, they have to learn that this test will be like nothing they have ever taken before. Their teacher who they love and is so kind and sweet, is going to say, 'Pencils down!' and mean it. They are not going to be able to raise their hands and say, 'Just another minute, I need time to finish.' You have to explain to them what a standardized test is.

Ideology

Education is perceived as an ideology and tests are perceived as a science; yet, society does not realize how tests in the name of science are introduced as an ideology. Tests have evolved from a situation in which they were a tool to become an ideology.

For ideas to become powerful and be put forward, they need to be recognized outside the circle of professionals and to converge with the strategies of groups outside the field. Thus, for tests to be powerful they needed to be recognized outside the field of professional testers or bureaucrats. This is the point at which the symbolic power of tests turns into ideologies. Specifically, it refers to myths about tests which are spread through propaganda and make people believe that tests are a condition for well being. It is at the point, when the rhetorics of tests are used for false information and propaganda, that tests are turned into an ideology.

Spolsky (1998: 1) notes that:

> For much of this century, the general public has been brain-washed to believe in the infallibility, fairness and meaningfulness of the results of tests and examinations. And not unnaturally, a large industry has developed that exploits this belief by selling tests and material to prepare for tests.

There is ample evidence to show how tests as power symbols are turned into ideologies. The rhetoric of testing is based on a variety of slogans and propaganda which spread various myths about testing. Part of the rhetoric of testing is the use of numbers. Numbers are very powerful for spreading and reinforcing ideologies and they are often more powerful than words. Tests have unchallenged authority and are considered to be the domain of experts, experts whom the public rarely dares to criticize or to challenge. Yet, the public is unaware that numbers are subjective, scientism is relative and success or failure, which is determined by arbitrary cutting scores, is open to different interpretations and can be challenged. Those working with statistics and numbers know how unreliable numbers can be, but those who are affected by numbers have trust in their power and authority.

The discourse of testing, then, spreads myths about tests that are believed by subjects of tests to be true. House (1998) points to the myths which are spread by authorities about the power of tests. Tests are described in magic terms mostly as tools capable of changing and improving everything in the education system. They can automatically create excellent achievements and raise standards. House points to statements used in *World Class Standards for American Education,* which provide evidence about the advantages and benefits of standards for parents. It states that tests and standards will raise achievements of *all* (my emphasis) students, raise expectations, expand learning in school and at home and will introduce equality as well as efficiency. Below are some examples that relate both to tests and to standards:

> The purpose of having standards is to raise the achievement of all students and to ensure that all students have equal opportunity.
>
> Having good standards means setting higher expectations for students. Students will learn more when more is expected of them, in school and at home . . .
>
> In the absence of national standards, a haphazard national curriculum has evolved based on standardized multiple-choice tests and mass market textbooks . . . When no one agrees on what students should learn, then each part of the education system pursues different, and sometimes contradictory goals. As a results, the education system as a whole riddled with inequity, incoherence, and inefficiency.
>
> (House, 1998: 27–8)

What is remarkable in these statements is how much weight is being granted to tests and how they are being 'sold' to naive parents by professional educators as being the instruments that can bring about massive, intensive and instant change in all aspects of education. They will affect textbooks, understanding, develop problem-solving and reasoning abilities, raise teacher quality, promote high standards, as well as introducing new technologies.

- Textbooks will change to emphasize student understanding.
- Student assessment will change to test whether students understand what they have learned.
- Instructional methods will change to emphasize reasoning and problem-solving.
- Teacher education will change and professional development will change so that all teachers are prepared to teach to higher standards.
- New technologies will be used to increase learning to meet the new standards.

(House, 1998: 28)

House notes that if any other product used in western society had been promoted, marketed and advertised in such a way, it would be the subject of major law suits, as none of these claims has any empirical support. Yet, with regard to tests these claims are not being questioned by anyone, which clearly explains why they are being accepted by the naive public. Clearly, no evidence is being presented about inaccuracies, danger or misuses of tests.

In the example of President Clinton, the ideology of testing is being sold as false promises, similar to those in an election campaign. Thus, the public is led to accept simplistic notions about education. It is specifically stated that the only conditions for success are about setting high level goals, nothing is said about how they will be achieved:

when we aim high and challenge our students, they will be the best in the world.

Similar false expectations are being raised by the Governor of Massachusetts with regard to the teacher certification, as quoted in Chapter 11, pp. 91–3:

'Every parent I talked to said, "We want the high standards",' he said today in a telephone interview. 'As I said at the Board of Ed meeting, I started off quoting John Kennedy when he said 36 years ago: "We choose to go to the moon and do other things, not because it's easy but because it's hard." And no one ever said improving our public schools would be easy. It is hard. There will be controversy and there will be conflict and there will be stumbles, but if we stick with it, we'll get there, and the best way to get there is to hold the line on standards.'

Yet another example in Chapter 8, p. 51 is the one given by the Ministry of Education with regard to the educational values of national assessment tests.

It will help the schools plan their work for the following year. The results will be used by the Ministry for pedagogical purposes only, for follow up, for research and for establishing policy. The data will be confidential and kept in the data base of the Ministry of Education.

Conclusions

Tests represent symbolic power and ideologies. The enhancement of tests as symbols is performed both by those in power and by those who are subject to the tests and who grant them with the power that they can then exercise. It is an unwritten contract between the two that is used to perpetuate the existing social order. The symbolic power of tests is enhanced via a number of mechanisms – using the tests to determine rite of passage, socializing children from an early age and thus creating the dependence of tests as the index of self worth, granting tests economic values, using ceremonial features, and controlling the content and texts of the tests. In a more radical form, tests turn from symbols to ideologies when myths and false assumptions are spread to create an even more powerful domination.

Part

IV

Democratic perspectives of testing

What steps should society take to limit, minimize and control such powerful uses of tests as described in this book? This last part of the book will propose strategies, solutions and alternatives for monitoring and controlling the powerful uses and misuses of tests and for practising more democratic strategies.

Chapter 16 introduces the notion of critical testing, referring to the need to examine the uses and consequences of tests and to limit and control their powerful uses. An integral part of critical testing is the introduction of democratic ways of assessment. Chapter 17 proposes such democratic principles and practices using alternative assessment and interactive/dialogical strategies; Chapter 18 discusses the social responsibilities of the testers; and Chapter 19 provides test takers with a method of protecting their rights. Chapter 20 is an epilogue that examines the future of testing, given society's competing ideologies.

16

Critical language testing

Critical testing: main features

Viewing tests as powerful tools – embedded in social and political contexts and agendas, related to intentions, effects and consequences and open to interpretations and values – places the field of testing within the broad area of *critical pedagogy* and is referred to here as *critical testing*.

Critical testing implies the need to develop critical strategies to examine the uses and consequences of tests, to monitor their power, minimize their detrimental force, reveal the misuses, and empower the test takers. It refers to the activity of embedding tests in reference to social, ethical, educational and political contexts. It attempts to provide a critique of the field of testing and make testers more aware and more socially reflexive by collecting data on the uses of tests as well as by pointing out such uses to users and the public at large. Its most important aims, in reference to the findings of this book regarding the uses of tests, are to minimize, limit and control the powerful uses of tests. It further attempts to encourage testers, teachers, test takers and the public at large to question the uses of tests, the materials they are based on and to critique their values and the beliefs inherent in them.

The following (adapted, in part, from Pennycook, 1994, and Kramsch, 1993) are the principles that are proposed as making up critical testing:

- Critical testing claims that the act of language testing is not neutral. Rather, it is a product and agent of cultural, social, political, educational and ideological agendas that shape the lives of individual participants, teachers and learners.
- Critical testing encourages test takers to develop a critical view of tests as well as to act on it by questioning tests and critiquing the value which is inherent in them.
- Critical testing views test takers as political subjects in a political context.

- Critical testing views tests as tools directly related to levels of success, deeply embedded in cultural, educational and political arenas where different ideological and social forms are in struggle.
- Critical testing asks questions about what sort of agendas are delivered through tests and whose agendas they are.
- Critical testing claims that testers need to ask themselves what sort of vision of society tests create and what vision of society tests are used for. Are tests merely intended to fulfil predefined curricular or proficiency goals, or do they have other agendas?
- Critical testing examines calls for a need to question the purposes and actual uses of tests. Are they intended to measure and assess knowledge or are they used to define and dictate knowledge?
- Critical testing asks questions about whose knowledge tests are based on. Is what is included in language tests 'truth' to be handed on to test takers, or is it something that can be negotiated, challenged and appropriated?
- Critical testing examines the stakeholders of tests. Are tests the product and creation of testers alone, or do they involve other stakeholders in a more democratic and involved process, who have an equal voice in the construction and use of tests, such as policy makers, test writers, students parents and teachers?
- Critical testing perceives testing as being caught up in an array of questions concerning education and social systems. The notion of 'just a test' is an impossibility because it is impossible to separate language testing from the many contexts in which it operates.
- Critical testing admits that the knowledge of any tester is incomplete and that there is a need to rely on additional sources to obtain a more accurate and valid description and interpretation of knowledge.
- Critical testing challenges psychometric traditions and considers interpretive ones whereby different meanings and interpretations are considered for test scores, with no attempt made to arrive at an absolute truth.
- Critical testing considers the meaning of language test scores, the degree to which they are prescriptive, final or absolute, and the extent to which they are open to discussion, negotiations and multiple interpretations.
- Critical testing challenges the knowledge on which tests are based. Is that knowledge limited to those in power who are eager to maintain and preserve their power and knowledge, or is it a democratic representation of the multiple groups in society?
- Critical testing challenges the uses of 'the test' as the only instrument to assess knowledge and considers multiple procedures, the sum of which can provide a more valid picture for interpreting the knowledge of individuals.

Critical testing thus broadens the field of language testing by engaging it in a wider sphere of social dialogue and debate about the forms and practices of testing to language teaching and language learning. This debate is surrounded by the roles that tests play and have been assigned to play in society, about competing ideologies, the discourse that is constructed and the roles of language testers. This debate draws testers towards areas of social processes and power struggles embedded in the discourses on learning and democracy.

Critical testing signifies a paradigm shift in testing in that it introduces new criteria for the validity of tests. Consequential, systemic, interpretive and ethical are a few of the new forms of validity, calling for the need to collect empirical data on the uses of tests. Such evidence may show that tests that were considered valid in the past, may not now be so if they are shown to have negative consequences and misuses in education.

The agenda for critical testing

Pennycook (quoted in McNamara, 1997) proposes additional directions with regard to the future agenda of critical language testing:

1. To make language testing a discipline and an area of knowledge that is reflexive and socially aware.
2. To conduct a critique of language testing as a disciplinary practice in a Foucauldian sense.
3. To provide a type of liberal response to such a critique by suggesting alternative types of testing.
4. To suggest the potential of language testing itself to have transformative effects on society.

Davies (1997: 328) notes that

> Critical approaches to language testing expose the importance of carefully examining alternative assessment proposals and making clear the validity of the assessment methods used by the profession.

One could claim that some of these agendas are already taking place. Specifically a number publications critical of language tests have recently appeared. These include the seminal book by Spolsky (1995), *Measured Words*, which examined the use of tests as political tools by authoritative testing agencies, two special issues of *Language Testing*, a number of encylopaedia items and a growing number of dissertations and research articles.

Critical testing needs to ask questions such as: Who are the testers? What is their agenda? Who are the test takers? What is their context? What is the context of the topic being tested? Who is going to benefit from the test? Why is the test being given? What will its results be used for? What is being tested and why? What is not being tested and why? What are the underlying values behind the test? What are the testing methods? What additional evidence is collected about the topic? What kind of decisions are reached based on the test? Who, excluding the tester, is included in the design of the test and its implementation? What ideology is delivered through the test? What are the messages about students, teachers and society that the test assumes? What type of feedback is being provided based on the test, and to whom? Can the test, its rationale and results be challenged? What are the intended and unintended uses of the test? What are its washback? What are some of the ways that test takers and others use to challenge the test?

The practice of critical testing is essential as there will always be those who will try to take control and avoid democratic processes. But the role of society is to protect itself from those who try to break it. Thus critical testing means applying procedures whereby society can protect itself from those who would misuse tests. As was observed in this book, tests are easy tools to misuse – a fact that was not recognized until now. Those who were responsible for tests had great authority and power to use them in different directions. Moreover, as was noticed by Bourdieu (1991), the use of tests for power and control, and for all kinds of reasons, was practised with the support and help of those being tested. Test takers actually granted unlimited power to testers.

Thus, critical testing argues that there is a need to examine the uses of tests critically, especially in terms of misuses, from the viewpoint of the test takers who are paying the price of such misuses in society; and to examine how groups, especially policy makers, take tests for granted and use them as they wish. The situation with language tests is even more intense as it builds on a double power – that of tests and that of language, especially the English language, implying therefore that language testers even more than other testers need to get involved in the practice of critical language testing.

There is a need to guard against misuses, to ask questions about uses, to examine unfair behaviour, and to suggest other ways of testing. Specifically in the area of power there is a need to make tests less authoritative and more democratic, to empower test takers and develop safeguards against misuses – and clearly not leave tests in the hands of bureaucrats. Testers need to realize that there is a need for responsibility; if they do not wish not take it, others will, and use it in more harmful and undemocratic ways.

Three areas of critical testing will be discussed in the remaining chapters of this book: collaborative approaches to assessment, Chapter 17; the social and ethical responsibility of the testers, Chapter 18; and the rights of the test taker, Chapter 19.

17

Collaborative approaches to assessment

Giroux (1995: 36) writes that democracy takes up the issue of

> transferring power from élites and executive authorities who control the
> economic and cultural apparatus of society, to those producers who yield
> power at the local level and is made concrete through the organization and
> exercise of horizontal power in which knowledge needs to be widely shared
> through education and other technologies of culture.

Darling-Hammond (1994) argues that there is a need to change the ways in
which we use assessment from sorting mechanisms to diagnostic supports;
from external monitors of performance to locally generated tools for enquir-
ing deeply into teaching and learning; and from purveyors of sanctions for
those already undeserved to levers for equalizing source.

Such approaches can be used as a basis for a democratic system of assessment of horizontal power in which knowledge and power are shared.

Sharing the power and constructing knowledge

Testing is practised nowadays as a reflection of knowledge and values of
those in authority, with very little attention given to the other interested
agents, test takers included. McNeil (1986) further states that accountability
and control schemes often generate the opposite of what they intend so that
when the school's organization becomes centred on managing and controlling, teachers and students take school less seriously. They fall into a ritual
of teaching and learning that tends towards minimal standards and minimal
efforts.

Yet, according to Giroux (1995), democratic systems of assessment are
based on principles whereby the power of tests is transferred from élite and

executive authorities who are presently in control to the local levels, test takers, teachers, students and parents.

Freire (1985) promotes an approach whereby a meaningful dialogical between two partners – the evaluator and the evaluatee – takes place. This is one way whereby evaluation is differentiated from inspection.

> Evaluation, that is, and not inspection. Through inspection, educators just become objects of vigilance by a central organization. Through evaluation, everyone is a subject along with the central organization in the act of criticism and establishing distance from the word. In understanding the process in this way, evaluation is not an act by which educator A evaluates educator B. It's an act by which educators A and B together evaluate an experience, its development, and the obstacles one confronts along with any mistakes or error. Thus, evaluation has a dialectical character. . . . It's essential that members of the evaluating organization deeply believe that they have as much to learn from educators directly linked to popular bases as those who study at the bases. Without this attitude, the evaluators from an external organization will never admit to any gap between their view of reality and reality. By believing they possess the truth, the evaluators act out their infallibility. And with such hypothesis, when they evaluated, they inspect.
>
> (Freire, 1985: 23–5)

Such approaches change the balance of powers of tester and test taker. Previously, testing followed the assumption that testers have all the knowledge of testing. Adopting democratic approaches assumes that the tester is no longer the 'know it all' owning all the knowledge, but rather that knowledge of measurement is so complex that even the best professional, familiar with all the advanced methods of testing, does not have all the answers.

Yet, Freire also claims that adopting such an approach requires members of the evaluating organization to believe deeply that they have as much to learn from educators directly linked to popular bases as those who study at the bases. Without such an attitude the evaluators from an external organization will never admit to any gap between their view of reality and reality itself. Believing they possess the truth, the evaluators remain sure of their infallability. And with such a hypothesis, when they evaluate, they inspect.

Current views, therefore, perceive the act of testing as a mutual effort of testers and test takers along with other sources of knowledge (parents, teachers, peers). Together, they construct the assessment knowledge by trying to make sense of the knowledge in a dialogical and co-operative way. In this process the tester admits his or her limitations and creates the assessment knowledge in a responsible way by working together with a number of agents who can provide evidence of the knowledge. Freedman (1993) also joins the argument that reformers must begin by working collaboratively with schools and the communities they serve, involving teachers, administrators, students and parents.

Fetterman, Kaftarian and Wandersman (1996) introduce the notion of *empowerment evaluation* to refer to a collaborative approach to evaluation which fosters improvement and self-determination and aims to help people to help themselves and improve their programmes using a form of self-evaluation and reflection. Accordingly, programme participants conduct their own evaluation and the evaluator typically acts as facilitator and collaborator rather than expert and counsellor. The professional evaluator works with the participants and thus becomes a resource in evaluation. They claim that such an approach is fundamentally democratic as it invites participation, examining issues of concern to the entire community in an open forum.

Thus, the new models of assessment that are currently proposed follow principles of shared power, collaboration and representation, and can therefore be viewed as more democratic. In some approaches, local groups – test takers, students, teachers and schools – share power by collecting their own assessment evidence using multiple assessment procedures (portfolios, self-assessment, projects, observations and tests). These procedures then provide evidence which is indicative of the knowledge of those whose knowledge is being assessed. The professional tester serves mostly as a facilitator who assists in the strategies of collecting the information and in the interpretation.

In some extreme models all the power is transferred from central bodies to local ones. Such is the case, for example, when external examinations are abolished in favour of local and internal assessment. Yet, such an approach is often criticized as the power relationship is being transferred to the teacher who may engage in undemocratic behaviour in the classroom. Broadfoot (1996) demonstrates how, in some situations, such approaches may lead to an illusion of democracy, as teachers become the new servants of the central systems, referred to by her as 'a new order of domination' (p. 87).

The preferred model is therefore a democratic one, where power is not *transferred* but rather *shared* with local bodies collaboratively based on a broader representation of different agents, central and local who, together, go through a process of contextualization of the evidence obtained from the different sources. Through constructive, interpretive and dialogical sessions each participant collects language data and demonstrates it in an interpretive and contextualized manner. This approach can then be applied in the national, district or classroom context and suggests, therefore, that assessment of students' achievement ought to be seen as an art, rather than a science, in that it is interpretive, idiosyncratic, interpersonal and relative.

There are a number of examples that demonstrate the use of such a model.

Moss (1996) gives the example of contextualization and shared authority with regard to certification. In this model the decision about certification is made locally, through dialogue among those professionals who are familiar with the candidates and/or with contexts in which the candidates work (p. 25). She suggests that '[t]he evaluation might not only be based on the portfolio but also on documented observations and interactions over time with the candidate. There, the state or other outside evaluators would assume more of an auditing role to ensure that the process would be equitable, reflect state or professional standards, and be sufficiently rigorous to protect the public from the licensure of incompetent professionals' (p. 25).

Experimenting with another model of assessment in the area of immigrant students acquiring a new language, Shohamy (1995) reports on a democratic assessment model. In that model the language proficiency of the immigrants is being assessed by a number of agents – teachers, who collect data via tests and observations; the test takers themselves, who provide evidence of their language performance through self-assessment and portfolios; and a standardized diagnostic test administered by a central body. The information obtained from all these agents through the various instruments is then gathered, processed and interpreted in an assessment conference, where language teachers, classroom teachers, students and occasionally parents, discuss and interpret the information leading to meaningful recommendations for pedagogical strategies of language improvement. In this case the assessment follows democratic principles of sharing and dialoguing and is also useful for improving language proficiency.

Nevo (1996) applies a similar dialogically shared model in programme evaluation and lists principles that underlie such a dialogical model. Accordingly, dialoguing implies a two-way relationship that is based on the assumption that nobody knows everything, but both parties know something and through dialogue they will learn more. Dialoguing implies a willingness of both parties to understand, and it acknowledges that each side has limitations. Dialoguing is a continuous process based on information that must be data driven and is relevant. In such a form of evaluation each part is responsible for consequences.

In the model of empowerment evaluation introduced by Fetterman et al. (1996), which focuses on self-determination and collaboration, the evaluation is a group activity, not an individual pursuit. It invites participation, examining issues of concern to the entire community in an open forum leading to deep insight into the programme. Programme participants learn to continually assess their progress towards self-determined goals and to reshape their plans and strategies according to this assessment. The evaluator teaches ways to conduct self-evaluation to enable it to become more efficient. They claim that such an approach desensitizes and demystifies evaluation and helps organizations internalize evaluation principles and practices, making it an integral part of programme planning. The claim is that an evaluation conducted by programme participants is designed to be ongoing and internalized in the system, creating the opportunity for capacity building.

Howe (1994), also supports such types of democratic models as providing a viable alternative by requiring the inclusion of 'voices that have historically been excluded in negotiating educational goods *worth wanting*' (p. 30). Lynch (1997) argues that such a view ensures each individual can participate effectively in the political process of society and on the personal level can achieve a sense of self-esteem. Howe is, therefore, not objecting to large-scale assessment to monitor outcomes under a democratic framework, but cautions against the use of assessment and standards as the *solution* (my emphasis) to learning problems.

The application of such models in the classroom is especially relevant as it provides students with the experience of democratic assessment behaviour from an early age. Students and teachers provide evidence that is indicative of language performance, to be discussed and evaluated in a conference between them. Such democratic practices in the classroom are especially useful as children become adults and become aware of the need to guard and protect their rights from the assessment machinery of centralized bodies.

It is obvious that such methods must be more time consuming and costly. However, democratic practices are not chosen for their efficiency or cost; rather they are chosen because of their principles. This is why central bodies, and testing factories, always make efforts to reject such proposals.

Alternative paradigms

One area that is receiving special attention in the literature is that of alternative paradigms of testing. Moss (1996) argues for a need to expand the dialogue among measurement professionals to include voices from research traditions different from the conventional ones. She proposes a critical dialectic between a naturalist conception of social science, from which the tradition of educational measurement has evolved, and an interpretive conception of social science.

In traditional mode the interpretations are predetermined by the score. The interpretive mode argues, however, that the methods and goals are inadequate to represent social phenomena. Specifically, this is because the object domain of social science is made up of largely symbolic constructions – texts, products, performances and actions – that reflect the meanings, intentions and interpretations of individuals who produce and receive them. This implies that social scientists cannot comprehend a human action by taking an outside observer position, but rather they must seek to understand what the actors mean by their actions. Further, Moss notes that the interpretations that social scientists construct can be reinterpreted and integrated into the lives of the subjects they describe. There is a need, therefore, to understand the meaning in the context in which it is produced and received, i.e. in light of the particular cases it is intended to represent.

Moss (1996: 20) concludes, therefore, that:

> The dialectic implied in such a reciprocal critique, particularly when under-taken with the respectful intent of comprehending the alternative perspective as fully as possible (Bernstein, 1982), provides a generative model through which assessment theory and practice can evolve.

Multiple assessment procedures

One important component within democratic approaches is the considera-tion of multiple sources of evidence of the construct being measured. This is based on the assumption that tests are limited in what they can assess and that it is therefore essential that other procedures will be used to get to those areas that cannot be tapped by tests. Therefore, other sources of evidence should be used before making detrimental judgements about individuals. Spolsky (1998: 10) notes:

> Rather than expecting some simple mechanical device to translate the complex data of individual language proficiency into a single measure, language testers too would benefit from intelligent and responsible 'inter-pretations drawn from patterns evident among the combined measures'.

Freedman (1993) shows how portfolio assessment in the assessment of writing can provide new links between large-scale testing and classroom assessment. She claims that if we could create a tight fit between large-scale testing and classroom assessment, we could potentially add to the kinds of information we now get from large-scale testing programmes and could help teachers to strengthen their classroom assessments, their teaching and their students' learning. Similarly, the example mentioned above by Shohamy (1995) in testing immigrant children is based on multiple sources of evidence which are indicative of the language proficiency of the immigrant children.

The use of feedback

One more democratic approach is the use of tests as learning tools rather than as power tools. This means that tests are very useful tools for providing meaningful information which can be incorporated into the education sys-tem. From an ethical perspective this is a very useful approach, as using tests for power and control, and not providing the test taker with feedback, can be considered as a situation in which the test taker is being used by those in authority. In such ways the test taker becomes a tool through which the agenda of those in power can be achieved but the test taker receives no personal benefit. Thus, the use of feedback provides a more ethical and pedagogical approach, as the outcome is improved learning.

It was mentioned earlier that when policy makers use tests as a means for shaping educational policies they are in fact using test takers as the ammunition in that battle. Yet, the test takers in most situations, do not benefit whatsoever from the testing. In all the three tests described in Chapters 8 to 10, the test takers received no feedback that could have been used to improve their learning. Often students obtain no information and they are left to speculate on what they did wrong and why they failed or succeeded on a test. Often students feel that they passed a test successfully and are later informed that they did not, without ever finding out why. This is a very unsatisfactory situation when the criteria for success remain hidden from the test takers. Yet, feedback from tests is the minimum that testers need to supply to test takers. The feedback should be used to expand and get to deeper insight into learning.

The question, then, is: How can tests be used to maximize their role as a means for obtaining information relevant to the improvement of learning, while at the same time minimizing their power and control roles?

Especially in situations when tests are used for policy making, testers have the responsibility to provide test takers with meaningful feedback that can be constructive in improving their learning. For example, in the reading comprehension test, there is a lot of information that may be used as feedback, thus giving a score of pass or fail is clearly insufficient in this case.

There is a need, therefore, to rely less on the power of tests and put more emphasis on the useful information that tests can provide for the improvement of teaching and learning. It is possible, for example, to use tests to supply decision makers (students, teachers and administrators) with valuable information and insights on teaching and learning. The information obtained from tests, when it is relevant and innovative, can provide evidence of teachers' performance, of students' ability over a whole range of skills, subskills and dimensions, and of students' achievement and proficiency on a continuous basis and in a detailed and diagnostic manner. According to Nitko (1989, 1996) information that is innovative and meaningful can lead to utilization. Such information can be useful for judging students in relation to the expectations outlined in the curriculum, to determine whether the school as a whole is performing well in relation to other schools that share the same curricula, to determine whether the teaching methods and textbooks used are effective tools for achieving those goals, and to determine whether the goals are realistic and appropriate. It is the information obtained from tests and its utilization which should make them valuable and powerful. When decision makers realize the value of the information that tests provide, improvement can result. Information can be utilized properly, especially when teachers – who are expected to carry out the changes – are involved in the assessment process. Once conclusions are reached on the basis of this information, it is possible to align the curriculum with the information and to implement changes in goals, teaching methods and textbooks. These changes can then be monitored through repeated administration of tests on an ongoing basis.

Fredriksen and Collins (1989) contend that information obtained from tests can contribute to improved learning when tests are connected to the learning that takes place in the classroom. They introduce the notion of systemic validity to refer to the introduction of tests, together with a whole set of variables which are part of the learning and instructional system. Accordingly, the introduction of tests is a dynamic process, in which changes in the education system take place according to feedback obtained from tests. In systemic models, a valid test is one that brings about, or induces, an improvement in the tested skills after a test has been in the education system for a period of time. Fredriksen and Collins contend that high systemic validity can only be achieved when a whole set of assessment activities foster it. They identify such activities as the use of direct tests, practising self-assessment procedures, repeated testing, feedback on test performance and multiple levels of success. They claim that the efficiency of current testing practices is greatly outweighed by the cost of using a system that has low systemic validity – one that has a negative impact on learning and teaching, since the goal of testing has to be to support the improvement of learning and teaching. Thus, tests that are used for the purpose of improving learning can be effective when they are connected to, and integrated into, other elements which are part of the education system and not when they are used in isolation.

18

Responsibilities of testers

It was argued in Chapter 2 that test takers have blind trust in, and fear and respect for, tests. Test takers have a feeling that they are in the hands of the testers and that tests and testers have total control over them in the testing situation. They further claim that testers are capable of manipulating situations over which they, the test takers, have no control. It is clear that testers and those who introduce tests are very powerful.

As was noted in Chapter 15, the symbolic power of those in authority is not just taken but in fact is granted by those who are subject to that power. Bourdieu argues that there is an unwritten contract between those in authority, and those who are subject to the authority, to maintain the power of tests as it serves both groups. In terms of the subjects, it helps them to maintain social order, perpetuate their role in society and grant those in authority with unlimited, almost magical power. Bourdieu (1991: 125–6) writes:

> He [the one in power] is what everyone believes him to be because his reality – whether priest, teacher or minister – is based not on his personal conviction or pretension . . . but rather on the collective belief, guaranteed by the institution and made concrete through qualifications and symbols like stripes, uniforms, and other attributes. The marks of respect, such as those which consist in addressing people by their titles . . . are so many repetitions of the inaugural act of institution carried out by a universally recognized authority and therefore based on *consensus omnium*. They are as valid oaths of allegiance, proof of recognition on regarding the particular person to whom they are addressed, but above all regarding the institution which instituted him . . .

Now, given the uses and misuses of tests (as described in this book) by those in authority as well as by testers, and the statement that there is no neutral testing but rather that testing is embedded in political and ideological ideologies and contexts, what should the role of the tester be?

Davies (1997) observes that there is a growing feeling among scholars in testing that challenges the morality of testing both within and from outside the field. He remarks that in language tests there is a

> growing feeling among scholars in language testing that challenges as to the morality of language testing were increasing both within and outside the field.
>
> (p. 235)

> While the growing professionalization of language testing is perceived as a strength and a major contribution towards a growing sense of ethicality, the increase in commercial and market forces, as well as the widespread use of language assessment as an instrument in government policy, may pressure language testers into dangerous (and unethical) conduct.
>
> (p. 236)

Spolsky (1998: 13) observes a similar phenomenon:

> The real-world desires for easy answers set major ethical challenges to testers who know the complexity of the task of assessing language proficiency.

Davies (1997: 235), therefore, poses some difficult questions about the ethics and morality of language testers:

> should testing specialists be responsible for decisions beyond test construction? Who decides what is valid? Does professionalism conflict with (1) public and (2) individual morality?

Language testers, Davies argues, have both professional and moral obligations. No social science is immune from such criticism, as it becomes less and less tenable for an academic discipline to allow their researchers the liberty to make up their own minds as to the conduct and practice of their professional research.

> There is urgent reason therefore both to examine the state of ethics in academic language testing and language testing research and to encourage a move towards an explicit statement of good conduct and practice.
>
> (Davies, 1997: 330)

Specifically, he brings up topics which can create such conflicts such as the relationships with stakeholders, the relationship between bias and fairness, washback, the politics of gate-keeping and a conflict between fairness and face validity. Once testers become aware of misuses of tests in society they

are faced with serious dilemmas as to their professional roles and responsibilities. Is the test developer responsible for uses and misuses of tests? What
is the role of the tester once he or she notices misuses? Is the tester's role at
that point to warn against misuses or actually to take steps such as using
sanctions against misuses? Or perhaps the tester has no responsibility to
worry about the test takers after a test had been handed to the users.

Various perspectives regarding the responsibility of the tester will be
explored in this chapter. Yet, there is a need first to define 'the tester'. Such
a definition is needed as it relates directly to who is responsible.

Defining the language tester

While throughout the book references are made to 'the tester' or to 'the
language tester', this is not a monolithic concept. Is the tester the person
who writes the questions and tasks of the test? Or perhaps it is the policy
maker who makes the decision to introduce a test to a system? Is it a government agency which funds the testing operation? Or is it the principal who
decides to administer the test in his or her school? Is it the researcher who
writes the test? Or is it the researcher who administers the test in order to
obtain information to answer some important research questions? Is it the
classroom teacher who writes a test and administers it to his or her students?
Or do the parents put pressure on school systems to have their children
tested by a standardized test?

The answer probably lies in all of the above, and more. A tester may be
anyone who is involved with the test in any form – writing test items, computing the test statistics, the researcher, the test designers. 'The tester', then,
refers to all those who take part in the decisions and actions to make the
testing event, or the testing experience, happen. These include policy makers,
researchers, question writers, statisticians, groups that pay for the test,
language supervisors who make a decision to administer the tests, parents
who support or motivate the introduction of tests, or even presidents who
believe that tests will save their nations. 'A tester' then is all those who have
made some contribution to the act of testing; therefore they all have some
responsibility to society.

This view is in line with Hamp-Lyons (1997: 298) who noted that it is not
just the test developer who has responsibility but other bodies who take part
in the introduction of the tests:

> it is not only test developers whose work has 'impact'; it is also testing
> agencies who make policy and economic decisions about the kinds of testing
> to support and the kinds that will not be supported; it is textbook publishers,
> who make economic decisions about the kinds of textbooks teachers and

parents will buy to 'ensure' their children are ready for the test; it is school districts, boards and ministries of education, and national or federal governments who bow to pressure to account for the progress of pupils and the value added effect of education.

The responsibilities of the tester: five views

Now that the different bodies that represent 'the tester' have been identified, the specific responsibilities of the tester will be discussed.

(a) Ethical perspective

Davies argues for an ethical perspective of professional morality which is defined as a contract for the profession and the individual with the public, thereby safeguarding all three. Yet, such a contract cannot take place without clear dilemmas, such as ensuring a balance between a professional ethical code and the individual moral conscience and even raising questions about the right of the profession to exist. At the same time he argues for a limit on what is achievable in terms of responsibility of consequences:

> the apparent open-ended offer of consequential validity goes too far. I maintain that it is not possible for a tester as a member of a profession to take account of all possible social consequences. What can be done is the internal (technical) bias analysis and a willingness to be accountable for a test's fairness. In other words, limited and predictable social consequences we can take account and regard ourselves as responsible for.
>
> (Davies, 1997: 336)

(b) Making others aware

Another view, not necessarily in contradiction to the first, is that the only responsibility a tester has with regard to the use of tests is to *point out* to society the intentions, effects and consequences of tests. Accordingly, the role of the tester is to collect data about dimensions and aspects of use and make this information known and accessible to the users and the public at large. Such a view follows Foucault (1991: 12) in *Remarks on Marx* with regard to the role of the intellectual in the society:

> The role of the intellectual does not consist in telling others what they must do. What right would they have to do that? ... The job of an intellectual does not consist in molding the political will of others but rather to challenge the way we think. ... There is always something ludicrous in

philosophical discourse when it tries, from the outside, to dictate to others, to tell them where their truth is and how to find it. . . .

Spolsky (1998) notes that the danger of tests comes in their misuses, and that misuse is made more likely by our failure to continue to publicize their inevitable uncertainty, and by our slowness to study and incorporate into our work the user's perspective.

(c) All consequences

A different view is expressed by Hamp-Lyons (1997: 302) who argues that the role of the tester is broader and that the tester needs to accept responsibility for all consequences of which he or she is aware:

> The responsibility of the language testers is clear: we must accept responsibility for all those consequences which we are aware of. Furthermore, there needs to be a set of conditions and parameters inside which we are sure of the consequences of our work and we need to develop a conscious agenda to push outward the boundaries of our knowledge of the consequences of language tests and their practices.

(d) Impose sanctions

Yet another view is that the responsibility of the tester is not simply to collect data on intentions and effects and make the public aware of such findings, but also to impose sanctions, punish and forbid the use of tests which are misused and punish those who violate the standard of correct testing practices. This argument views the tester as responsible to the product, and the tester therefore has the obligation to forbid its use when it is found to be defective. According to this argument, constructing a test is identical to the manufacturing of other products in society. It is similar, for example, to the responsibility of a manufacturer in designing a defective car, a poisonous drug or engaging in malpractice. In these situations it is understood that the manufacturer has a responsibility to generate a high-level product, and failing to do so results in a penalty for damaged outcomes.

(e) Shared responsibility and shared discourse

A different view follows the notion of shared responsibility – the responsibilities for good conduct are in the hands of all those who are involved in the testing process. In Chapter 17 it was proposed that there is a need to change the balance of power with regard to tests. The testers have previously had the authority of testing while the test takers were the passive objects, but calls are currently being made to change the balance of power by having the testers and test takers, and others who are involved in the process, share this authority. According to this view, shared authority also implies shared responsibilities. This view is based on the notion that testers need to admit that their knowledge is limited, that measuring knowledge by a single test administered by testing bodies cannot cover all domains of knowledge, and that the testers do not have all the answers when undertaking assessment. Thus, testers and test takers should engage in a mutually constructive effort, working together in constructing the meaning of knowledge. The responsibility of testers then, is to admit the limitations of their profession and construct knowledge in a responsible way, by working together with a number of groups of users who accumulate evidence of the knowledge that is being assessed. The responsibility also means using a variety of critical testing methods, such as those presented in Chapter 16 in discussing critical testing. Specifically, here it implies the need to be critical about tests and their uses, to collect data on the effects and consequences of tests, to warn against misuses, and to protect all those involved in the acts of testing – testers as well as test takers. It should be viewed as the responsibility of all to work for better instruments and uses of tests and to warrant against misuses.

Madaus (1990) claims that there is a need for people from outside the testing community to address the social, technical and value issues associated with testing. Specifically, he notes that this suggestion is not limited to the involvement of scientists or technicians from other communities but rather to extend it to the wider non-technical communities.

Thus, the responsibility for collecting data about the quality of the instruments as well as their uses is not only the responsibility of the testers but also of those with whom the tests are used and on whom the tests have an effect (intended or not). These include test takers as well as others who are responsible for civil and fair behaviour in society, e.g. courts and human rights groups. Although it is expected that testers will carry out some of this research, they are clearly less motivated to do so as often the results of their studies are not trusted. It is often noticed that there is low trust on the part of the public with regard to research conducted by companies that also develop and market tests, in a similar way that there is low trust in research conducted by profit-making drug companies on the drugs they produce. Clearly, research is trusted more when it is performed by independent groups. Thus, it is recommended that research on consequences should be performed by test takers, human rights activists and others in the society who are affected by test results. After all it is the role of society to defend itself from powerful institutions. It is therefore only logical that others, not only the testers, should be motivated to carry out research in order to defend themselves. After all, it is not expected that those who develop tests will be the sole bodies to carry out that research and examine its consequences.

It is therefore suggested here that research on the use of tests should be conducted in collaboration with other stakeholders. It is essential that testers

co-operate with experts not involved in testing and acquaint all those concerned with tests and their use with the vocabulary of testing. This process
will enable others to enter the discourse without being dismissed as naive,
thus improving communication between groups and having more people
outside the testing community address the social and technical values of
testing. This is also related to the need for shared discourse and for specify-
ing the type of information that needs to be collected.

A related issue to the shared responsibility is the shared discourse. Madaus
(in press: 6) notes that there has been a tense relationship between the testing community and lay people:

> It is certainly true that a gulf has developed between the testing commun-
> ity and others. In testing as in other technological areas, 'there is almost
> no middle ground of rational discourse, no available common language
> with which persons of differing backgrounds can discuss matters of tech-
> nology in thoughtful, critical terms . . .'

> (Winner, 1986, p. 11)

Madaus therefore claims that an additional responsibility of testers is to
acquaint all groups who have concerns about tests and their use with the
techniques and vocabulary of the testing community so that they can enter
into the discourse without being dismissed as naive. There is a need

> to improve communication between groups, words in the common lexicon
> that have been appropriated and narrowed by the testing fraternity need to
> be abandoned so that we no longer talk on parallel non-intersecting tracks.

> (p. 7)

The type of information needed

Adopting any of the above views regarding the types of responsibilities –
whether it is to make the public aware of the sanction, or the shared responsibility – requires the collection of data about the use of tests. Thus, a relevant issue concerns the types of data that need to be collected.

As was argued in Chapter 1, traditional testing does not focus on the uses
and consequences of tests, yet it should be clear by now that such information is crucial for upgrading the quality of tests. Thus, the responsibility of
the tester is to collect data about the quality of the instrument – the types of
reliability and validity relevant for the different users and adopted to different needs. This also includes the use of multiple ways of disseminating
information, including scores such as diagnostic information, comparisons,

profiles, verbal descriptors, narratives, progress profiles, interpretive sum-maries and more. It also includes information about the use of a test, such as intentions and rationales for introducing the test, long- and short-term effects on test takers, education and society, and other relevant information regard-ing the consequences of the test.

Professional morality

Davies brings up the topic of professional morality, which relates to the moral and ethical concerns that testers face once the field of testing encompass the use and consequences of tests.

Davies (1997: 328) notes the need for professional morality in addition to public and individual moralities. The testing profession, he claims, establishes contracts with the public but at the same time must protect its members. He quotes House (1990), claiming that 'ethics are the rules or standards of right conduct or practice, especially the standards of a profession'. Thus, he claims, it is important for all stakeholders, both inside and outside the institutions, that professional standards of behaviour are stated explicitly, so that stake-holders know what is meant by right conduct and practice, and therefore what can and cannot be expected.

> Following critical theorists in other social sciences, critical applied lin-guists have been asking questions about the ethics of applied linguistics and whether an ideologically neutral study of applied linguistics is possible. And where critical applied linguistics goes, critical language testing follows. There is urgent reason therefore both to examine the state of ethics in academic language testing and language testing research and to encourage a move towards explicit statement of good conduct or practice.
>
> (Davies, 1997: 328–9)

Davies justifies the need for professional morality and provides examples of the type of issues of which it can focus:

> professional morality . . . provides a contract for the profession and the individual with the public, thereby safeguarding all three. Professional research of a social nature is likely to state the profession's ethical position on issues having to do with informed consent, a taboo on invasions of privacy, confidentiality, precautions against injury, and distress, covert methods of conducting research, and agreeing on conventions for writing and publishing.
>
> (p. 333)

On the other hand, Davies notes that members of the profession need protection as well, clearly without reaching overprotection (especially the kind that can be associated with an incestuous concern for the protection of members of the profession, by avoiding and covering up complaints and offences to avoid legal actions in a climate of increasing litigation). After all, there have already been cases, and surely there will be more, when public assessment provides for potential complaints and legal actions because of the use of assessment in selection and certification. Those excluded or rejected often believe that the methods of assessment used were not valid and were, therefore, wrongly excluded or rejected. Thus, safeguards for professional practitioners are needed.

Standards for professional behaviour

One strategy of focusing on these issues is by developing standards of 'professional behaviours' which are expected to protect both the tester as well as the test taker.

Nevo and Shohamy (1986) introduced an adaptation they made of the *Standards for Evaluation of Educational Programs, Projects and Materials* (1981). These standards had been developed over a number of years by the Joint Committee on Standards for Educational Evaluation, made up of members from the AERA, the APA, the NCME and nine other organizations. They were designed to give guidance to professionals involved in the evaluation of educational programmes, and it was hoped that the establishment of a common set of principles would help to upgrade the practice of educational evaluation. The Joint Committee developed a set of 30 standards, divided into four headings: 'utility standards', 'feasibility standards', 'properiety standards' and 'accuracy standards'. Alderson, Clapham and Wall (1995: 251) note the unique dimension of these standards:

> these standards show a stronger interest in the context of the testing situation and how the public views the test itself; the reports; and the effect of the test on the candidates, education and society. The political viability of a test (C-2: Testing is planned and conducted with anticipation of the different positions of various interest groups, so that their cooperation may be obtained) is an issue which does not appear in other sets of testing standards.

Nevo and Shohamy (1986) extended these standards to testing methods. From the Joint Committee's original 30 standards they produced a list of 23 that they suggested were suitable for testing methods. All the standards were re-worded so that they would apply to test methods rather than to evaluation programmes. The standards were organized as follows:

1. **Utility standards**   *The utility standards are intended to ensure that a testing method will serve the practical information needs of given audiences.*

    Utility assures that a test serves the practical information needs of a given audience; for example, it is concerned with the impact that tests may have on instruction and learning in the classroom, such as backwash effects. Also included are other utility factors such as finding the best ways for training testers and raters and for presenting test results. They are also concerned with tester credibility, information scope, justified criteria, report clarity, dissemination timelines and impact.

2. **Accuracy standards**   *The accuracy standards are intended 'to ensure that a testing method will reveal and convey technically adequate information on the educational achievement of those that are being tested'.*

    Thus accuracy assures that the test represents reliable and valid measurements, testing conditions, data analysis and objective reporting.

3. **Feasibility standards**   *Feasibility standards are intended 'to ensure that a testing method will be realistic, prudent and frugal'.*

    Feasibility relates to whether tests are feasible to administer within different contexts, whether they are conducted with the support of certain political groups, whether they produce information of sufficient value to justify their costs, and whether it is practical to train people to conduct such tests.

4. **Fairness standards**   *These are intended 'to ensure that a testing method is conducted legally, ethically, and with due regard to the welfare of tested individuals as well as those affected by test results'.*

    Fairness relates to whether the tests are conducted legally and ethically, as well as with care for the welfare of the respondents. Included are questions on whether the tests are based on materials that examinees are expected to know, if they are conducted so that the rights and welfare of human subjects are respected, if they are conducted fairly with regard to the strength and weaknesses of the individuals tested, and if test takers have a positive attitude towards the tests.

Nevo and Shohamy also note that each of these elements can be viewed as another dimension within the broader view of test validation. They tried the standards out on relevant professionals. They asked two groups to study the standards and use them to rank four alternative testing methods which were being considered for a new national matriculation examination. The first group consisted of policy makers who were supposed to make the final decision about which of the testing methods would be included in the new examination; the second group consisted of testing experts attending a language-testing conference. They also designed a sample test which contained all four of the testing methods under consideration. This was administered to 1,000 students to find out how the test performed in the real world, and also to provide a basis for assessing whether several of the new testing standards could be used to evaluate such testing methods.

It is important to note that Alderson and colleagues claim that not enough attention was paid in the adaptation to the political aspects of the original standard and that in the original document it was stated that:

> The evaluation should be planned and conducted with anticipation of the different position of various interest groups, so that their cooperation may be obtained, and that possible attempts by any of these groups to curtail evaluation operations or to bias or misapply the results can be averted or counteracted.
>
> (Alderson, Clapham and Wall, 1995: 56)

Thus, the original standards can be adapted to testing as well, by referring to the use of tests as political weapons and by ensuring that testers are aware of all the possible ways in which their tests can be misused so that they can pre-empt any wrongdoing. They specifically focus on a distinction with regard to the misuse of tests: whether misuse is as the result of ignorance or carelessness, or whether the parties may deliberately misuse information in the way that was implied in the standard above.

In making decisions about the quality of tests, consideration must be given to a whole set of validation questions, which are related not only to accuracy but also to test utility, feasibility and fairness. Empirical data need to be collected on each aspect of the test. Thus, there is more than one way to examine a test: different criteria and standards, such as those listed above, are needed to provide answers relating to the quality of tests.

ILTA codes of ethics

In the past few years a number of efforts have been taking place to promote the use of codes of practice in order to professionalize the field. These codes give guidance on how to act responsibly. Codes of ethics commonly cover such areas as the professional's role in society with regard to integrity, conflicts of interest, diligence and due care, confidentiality, and communication with clients and the public (Nitko, 1996). Recently there has been a growing awareness of the need for a code of practice for language testers that will consider not only the traits of the test but also its uses and consequences. Appendix A displays the Code of Ethics that was developed by the International Language Testing Association (ILTA) and adopted in March 2000 in Vancouver.

19

Rights of test takers

The issue of the 'rights of test takers' is relatively new; in the past and to a large extent at present, test takers have simply had no rights. In fact, as was noted in Chapter 1, the test taker in traditional testing was not of major concern, and was viewed mostly as a black box. The test taker was important only insofar as computing the psychometric traits of the test. It was understood that there was specific knowledge that the test taker should have, but that the body of knowledge was defined by those who wrote the tests and that the test taker was expected to comply with their decision.

Yet, as described in Chapter 2, test takers are the true victims of tests. They suffer badly from tests in this unequal power relationship between the test as an organization and the demands put on test takers. It is clear that those who are affected by the test results do not have the right to pursue or try to understand the inside secrets of tests.

It is being argued (Lo, 1997) that in the case of the English language, the combination of the power of English with the power of the test creates a situation whereby the test takers are in a powerless situation:

> the lack of power students have in this examination, together with the dominance of English in Hong Kong society and thus the importance of this particular exam, places students in positions where they are unlikely to challenge these roles or messages.

> (p. 33)

Yet, it is very rare that a test taker could protest, complain or claim that the test did not fit his or her knowledge or that he or she was not expected to master that knowledge. It has been understood that the test taker has to manipulate his or her knowledge by complying with the test. It is clear that testing was, and still is, a very specialized area that requires specialized expertise to be able to criticize or protest about its structure or results. As was noted, the public had blind trust in tests. It is considered a scientific area that requires particular knowledge and expertise. Clearly, the authority of tests has been accepted, with no questions asked.

A major feature of the power of tests is the fact that tests are administered by powerful institutions. Thus, in the interaction between a tester and a test taker it is the tester who has the power, the tester who makes all the important decisions – what to test, how to administer the test, how to score and rate it and how to deliver the results. The only numbers the test taker can refer to are those provided by the tester, and these can only be challenged if one has counter numbers, which are generally impossible to obtain. In such situations it is difficult to see how the powerless individual will have the courage and strength to protest and demand any rights.

Hanson (1993: 19) notes that:

> In nearly all cases test givers are organizations, while test takers are individuals. Test-giving agencies use tests for the purpose of making decisions or taking actions with reference to test takers – if they are to pass a course, receive a certificate, be admitted to college, receive a fellowship, get a job or promotion. That, together with the fact that organizations are more powerful than individuals, means that the testing situation nearly always places test givers in a position of power over test takers.

Furthermore, it is the tester who determines the information and the knowledge, that will be included in tests, and the information the test taker needs to comply with. It is a built-in system through which the testing organization – whether it is a school, education system, government or industry – has total control over that knowledge, which is non-negotiable and can provide a mechanism for continuous control over information and power. The knowledge included in tests is determined unequally and is dictated by those who plan and write the tests. It is this knowledge that can control, monitor and block the entrance of those who are not part of that knowledge.

Lo (1997) shows that the lack of power of the students in Hong Kong with regard to the English graduating test, together with the dominance of the English language in Hong Kong society, grants the test so much power that the students are placed in positions where they are unlikely to challenge these roles or messages. In her analysis, she also shows that the inferior place of the test taker on the test can already be noticed from the type of discourse and genres used in the instructions. These are written in a way that clearly shows that the test taker is looked down upon and is even placed in a confrontational situation with the Examination Authority. Students are described in the instruction as careless, lacking ideas and awareness and having 'problems', out of control and childish (pp. 39–40).

Thus, resentment of tests, in most cases, requires a lot of courage on the part of test takers to battle powerful testing organizations, especially in a high-stake test when results are so detrimental. This explains why individual test takers rarely appeal. There is a feeling on the part of individuals that there is just too much to lose.

Yet the growing involvement of the public in education in the past decade, and the increased power to litigate in a number of areas, has been extended to the area of testing as well. It is now realized by the public that while they may not know the statistical techniques for analysing tests, it is the uses of tests that count. It is therefore not uncommon to encounter situations where parents are resentful of tests and run campaigns to abolish them or to use them differently (Lynch, 1997).

There have been a number of court cases seeking legal redress for real and/or perceived violations of rights and this in turn brings testing pro-grammes to the court. Notable among legal issues are race or gender dis-crimination, unfairness and the violation of due process such as failure to give sufficient notice for a test or failure to give opportunities for hearings and appeals. Among the educational testing practices brought to court are minimum competence, teacher certification tests designed to control who is allowed to teach in a state, and college admissions testing. The most well-known case is that of *Debra P. et al.* v. *Turlington* (1979, 1981) which challenged Florida's minimum competency test.

What are the rights of the test takers?

The 'test taker' is defined here in a broader perspective rather than the individual who is taking the test. It is perceived as all those who are affected by the test results – for good or for bad. Thus, it includes the person who is actually taking the test, the teacher whose students are being tested, the prin-cipal whose school is being tested, and the parents whose children are taking a test. The common factor with all these groups is that they are affected by the results of the test in some way or another.

As was noted in Chapter 15, test takers are encouraged to develop a critical view of tests and to question their uses. It is therefore claimed that it is the right of test takers to question the test results and methods, in situa-tions where there is a feeling that the rights of the tester were violated. They may have been tested on unfamiliar material, using unfamiliar methods, and especially in situations when the test results were being used for purposes for which they were not intended. Testers, it is believed, should also have the right to refuse to be tested. Valdes and Figueroa (1996) claim that since the information obtained from tests used for bilinguals are uninterpretable, they propose to abolish all testing of circumstantial bilingual persons when such tests are used to select, certify, or guide interventions for individuals. It is realized, however, that this is a long process, given the present power of tests, which is in the hands of powerful institutions. Whether these are testing organizations, schools or teachers, it is difficult for the individuals to question and protest. A strategy that is recommended is the establishment of advocacy groups, the role of which is to protect test takers from powerful organizations. This is no different to malpractice as a result of bad medical treatment.

Punch (1994) brings up three aspects of what constitutes unethical or immoral outcomes of tests with regard to the test taker – consent, deception, and privacy and confidentiality.

- *Consent* refers to the individual's right to have a choice whether to be tested or not. It involves whether test takers have been clearly told that they are being tested, what they are being tested for and what will be done with the results of the testing.
- *Deception* refers to the notion of whether it is morally deceptive to have an individual engaged in an activity that he or she cannot clearly see as being directly related to the ability supposedly being tested. Thus, should the tester supply the test taker with information or practice sessions as to this unfamiliar method. Can the distractors in multiple-choice test format be thought of as deceptive by definition?
- *Privacy and confidentiality* refers to whether test takers are harmed by reporting results from a test that puts them at a certain place, that denies them entrance, that prevents them from accessing social and economic resources? Lynch stresses here that it is not the act of testing that is to blame, but certain realities in society call for selection based on merits and tests are efficient tools for such selection.

Test decisions/consequences and fairness

These terms refer to the difficulty of deciding what constitutes fairness. While decisions may be based on equal opportunities and conditions of testing, they do not imply that all test takers had equal opportunities to obtain an equal education. The rights of test takers can therefore be violated by having different educational backgrounds and, thus, the imposition of tests that are based on one type of knowledge, decided by some groups, is in violation of the rights of those test takers who come from different backgrounds.

Solutions

Some of the solutions to these dilemmas are suggested here. With regard to consent, a test taker should be given the right to be tested and the right to refuse to be tested. There should also be honesty with regard to the purpose of the test, its practice and methods. Next, a test taker should be granted the possibility of being assessed by an alternative method other than the traditional 'test-only' system. Such information can be used as counter evidence against decisions based on tests only. In addition, as was argued in Chapter 18, there is a need for sharing the power of tests by training the public in testing methods, in the testing process and in the rights of test takers. Testing cannot remain a field that belongs only to testers but rather test takers and the public at large need to be part of the discussion.

Two examples of a Code of Practice are displayed in Appendix B; they were drafted by parents in Australia and are similar to a Bill of Rights which attempts to define the rights of test takers and thus to protect them from the power of tests.

20

Epilogue

Tests have become tools which, in the name of objectivity, have created and perpetuated new subjective powers, and defined and dictated society's knowledge by building on the fear and trust of the public who are affected by their results. Tests have become tools which are used to perpetuate power and control, to screen and keep out those who are not part of the mainstream knowledge. Thus tests, originally developed for democratizing purposes, have become authoritative and centralized tools which are being manipulated in the hands of 'a few'.

This is perpetuated by the symbolic values of tests in most modern societies. Tests have become symbols of quality, standards, achievements and high-level order. Tests are being viewed as the equivalent to all of these terms; if there are tests then automatically one gains quality, standards and achievements. The rhetoric of testing is the key to public attention. Is there anyone who will object to high standards, to high quality and to achievements? What the public are not being told is that setting goals *per se* is no guarantee that they will be reached, and that there is a big gap between the two.

Tests are in the midst of a number of competing battles:

- Between the need of central agencies for control, and the desire for individual freedom.
- Between the urge of groups for a common unifying knowledge, and open and creative knowledge.
- Between a monolingual, one language for all, and multilingual tolerance.
- Between the public need for symbolic devices of social order, and the individual and group needs for personal expressions and freedom.
- Between increased control in growing technological societies, and fluid and relative knowledge.
- Between resentment of control by centralized agencies, and the need for control in order to maintain status and social order.
- Between practical concerns and ideological forces.

There are, therefore, different views with regard to the current state and future prospects of tests.

On the one hand, there are those who believe that the testing era is over, that there is no room for such authoritative tools in post-modern, multicultural societies where knowledge is relative and fluid, and where groups – linguistic and others – demand legitimacy, respect, identity and rights. Valdes and Figueroa (1996) argue for a radical yet equitable proposal in the context of bilingual testing. They propose a declaration of a national moratorium and suspension of all testing of circumstantial bilingual persons when such testing involves decision making about individuals. They claim that tests provide uninterpretable information and have far-reaching implications for these individuals in selection, certification, or any interventions. Instruments which are based on the standardization of an entire population – of all people, using the same criteria – pose major obstacles to self-expression. This view is reinforced nowadays when it is public knowledge that tests cannot measure knowledge accurately, and are misused and abused by authoritative powers for promoting agendas and maintaining the power of élites.

On the other hand, there are those who hold contrary views. They believe that tests will and should continue to exist – and have more power and control than ever. After all, tests can be the most beneficial tools for opposing those who demand to share power and to legitimize multicultural post-modern agendas. For example, it may be easy to fight the proponents of Ebonic with standardized English tests. Similarly, it is possible to fight bilingual education by introducing uniform English tests as the criterion for entrance and acceptance as part of the 'English Only' agenda.

Broadfoot is even more far reaching in her view of the future of tests. She argues that it is the combination of technology and bureaucracy that will enable central groups to further increase their power as they

> move[s] away from overtly political judgments about educational policy in favor of a technocratic ideology which legitimizes policy decisions in terms of an objective, rational process of decision making leading to the growing powerlessness of the individual to resist the effects of an increasingly intrusive state machinery.
>
> (Broadfoot, 1996: 217–18)

Yet, there is another view, which claims that tests are here to stay but in different shapes and forms. Such a view builds on the true power of tests – that of offering pedagogical benefits in a form of feedback, leading to more effective learning and teaching. This means that tests, as well as other assessment procedures, can be used not only for beneficial and constructive purposes but also to guard against central bodies and authoritative agencies who seek ways to use tests in unethical and undemocratic ways for power and control.

Tests have grown from being a 'means to an end' into being an end in themselves, from being the instrumental ideology to being the expressive ideology. It is therefore important not to be naive and to realize that none of these suggested models offers a real solution. There will always be those who will attempt to retain their dominance by continuing to use tests as part of the ongoing power struggle between individuals and groups and by using terms such as 'standards', 'quality', 'indicators' and other symbols of social order.

Madaus (1990) states that he does not see an end in sight to the rule of testing. Testing has become a defining technology capable of promoting as well as diminishing values. Moreover, it is a way by which people explain themselves to others. He notes that testing has achieved so much momentum and power that our society could experience grave difficulty if it were abolished. It is accepted without thought and is seen by society as a solution to a problem. The idea that a new test can reform schools and restore competitiveness is a technological fix which diverts attention from systemic problems in education. The danger, Madaus further claims, is that technological consciousness can lead to a neglect of moral, aesthetic and artistic consciousness. He makes an appeal to evaluate tests, as we should evaluate all important technologies; not only for their contribution to bureaucratic goals of efficiency, competitiveness and productivity, but also for the ways in which they can promote specific values and social relations, and diminish others.

The message conveyed in this book should not be interpreted in anarchistic terms. It is not a call for the abolishment of tests altogether; rather, it is a call for the practice of quality tests which, in the terms of this book, imply also the practice of democratic testing. Such testing requires shared authority, collaboration, involvement of different stakeholders – test takers included – as well as meeting the various criteria of validity. Following such procedures will lead to responsible testing. In simple terms this means: 'Do it, but do it with care'. Along with that there is a need for continuous examination of the quality of tests, for in-depth insight into how they are used, for the public exposure of misuses and for the awareness of the public as to the motivations for, harm and consequences of tests. The cost of this approach is high – it takes more time, it involves more people, it requires greater resources. It requires compromise as all democratic practices do. But, if tests are so central, yet they pose such strong potential for misuses, the cost is worth paying.

This is the challenge that testers need to face. Specifically:

- How can such testing practices be carried out?
- What are some of new methodologies that have to be developed in order to follow such practices?
- How can more democratic testing be pursued and, at the same time, guard the validity of the tests?
- How can test users be convinced not to use tests that do not meet such requirements?

For testers who now realize that the products they create are the means for such struggles, this poses a threat to the ethicality of the profession. Testers, therefore, must become engaged in the discussion. They must assume an active role in following the consequences and uses of tests, help to guard against misuses, and offer assessment models which are more educational, democratic, ethical, yet at the same time valid. There is ample evidence that tests are not neutral tools and, as such, testers cannot remove themselves from a test's intentions, effects and consequences. Therefore, they must also reject the notion of neutral and objective testing and offer alternative models of assessment to fight such uses. Pretending that tests are neutral allows those in power to misuse them. Testers must realize that much of the strength of tests lies not only their technical quality but in their use in social and political dimensions. Studies of the use of tests, as part of test validation on an ongoing basis, are essential for the integrity of the profession. The unique trait of *language* testers (as opposed to general testers) is their expertise in the subject matter – language learning. As such, they can become agents capable of bridging language learning, language testing and language use. Responsibly used, tests are an important source of information.

It is important for policy makers as well as for the public to pay attention to the values that testing promotes and those that it diminishes. Attention must also be given to such values as ethicality, equity and fairness.

A focus on the language-testing policies of nations as well as of education systems should also be of special concern to those working in the area of language policy. Research of the language-testing policies of countries and systems can provide a rich source for understanding of *de facto* language policies of nations and systems – beyond intentions, nice words and politically correct documents. The extent to which language-testing policies actually reflect language policies is an area that calls for research which can provide indications as to the validity of language policies.

As was shown in this book, language tests – like languages – provide a reflection, a mirror, of the complexities and power struggles of society. They lie at the crossroads of many conflicts and therefore should be studied, protected and guarded as part of the process of preserving and perpetuating democratic cultures, values and ethics, as well as the quality of learning. It is an important challenge for language testers, applied linguists and policy researchers in the years to come.

Appendix A

Code of Ethics for ILTA

(adopted at the annual meeting of ILTA held in Vancouver, March 2000)

This, the first Code of Ethics prepared by the International Language Testing Association (ILTA), is a set of principles which draws upon moral philosophy and serves to guide good professional conduct. It is neither a statute nor a regulation and it does not provide guidelines for practice, but it is intended to offer a benchmark of satisfactory ethical behaviour by all language testers. It is associated with a separate Code of Practice (in progress). The Code of Ethics is based on a blend of the principles of beneficence, non-maleficence, justice, a respect for autonomy and for civil society.

This Code of Ethics identifies 9 fundamental principles, each elaborated on by a series of annotations which generally clarify the nature of the principles; they prescribe what ILTA members ought to do or not do, or more generally how they ought to comport themselves or what they, or the profession, ought to aspire to; and they identify the difficulties and exceptions inherent in the application of the principles. The Annotations further elaborate the Code's sanctions, making clear that failure to uphold the Code may have serious penalties, such as withdrawal of ILTA membership on the advice of the ILTA Ethics Committee.

Although this Code derives from other similar ethical codes (stretching back into history), it does endeavour to reflect the ever changing balance of societal and cultural values across the world, and for that reason should be interpreted by language testers in conjunction with the associated Code of Practice.

All professional codes should inform professional conscience and judgement. This ILTA Code of Ethics does not release language testers from the obligations and responsibilities laid on them by other Codes to which they have subscribed or from their duties under the legal codes, both national and international, to which they may be subject.

Language testers are independent moral agents and sometimes they may have a personal moral stance which conflicts with participation in certain procedures. They are morally entitled to refuse to participate in procedures which would violate personal moral belief. Language testers accepting employment positions where they foresee they may be called on to be involved in situations at variance with their beliefs have a responsibility to acquaint their employer or prospective employer with this fact. Employers and colleagues have a responsibility to ensure that such language testers are not discriminated against in their workplace.

The Code of Ethics is instantiated by the Code of Practice (currently under preparation by ILTA). While the Code of Ethics focuses on the morals and ideals of the profession, the Code of Practice identifies the minimum requirements for practice in the profession and focuses on the clarification of professional misconduct and unprofessional conduct.

Both the Code of Ethics and the Code of Practice need to be responsive to the needs and changes within the profession and, in time, these Codes will require revision in response to changes in language testing and in society. The Code of Ethics will be reviewed within five years, or earlier if necessary.

Principle 1

- Language testers shall have respect for the humanity and dignity of each of their test takers. They shall provide them with the best possible professional consideration and shall respect all persons' needs, values and cultures in the provision of their language testing service.

Annotation

- Language testers shall not discriminate against nor exploit their test takers on grounds of age, gender, race, ethnicity, sexual orientation, language background, creed, political affiliations or religion, nor knowingly impose their own values (for example social, spiritual, political and ideological), to the extent that they are aware of them.
- Language testers shall never exploit their clients nor try to influence them in ways that are not related to the aims of the service they are providing or the investigation they are mounting.
- Sexual relations between language testers and their test takers are always unethical.
- Teaching and researching language testing involving the use of test takers (including students) requires their consent; it also requires respect for their dignity and privacy. Those involved should be informed that their refusal to participate will not affect the quality of the language tester's service (in teaching, in research, in development, in administration). The use of all forms of media (paper, electronic, video, audio) involving test takers requires informed consent before being used for secondary purposes.
- Language testers shall endeavour to communicate the information they produce to all relevant stakeholders in as meaningful a way as possible.
- Where possible, test takers should be consulted on all matters concerning their interests.

Principle 2

Language testers shall hold all information obtained in their professional capacity about their test takers in confidence and they shall use professional judgement in sharing such information.

Annotation

- In the face of the widespread use of photocopied materials and facsimile, computerized test records and data banks, the increased demand for accountability from various sources and the personal nature of the information obtained from test takers, language testers are obliged to respect test takers' right to confidentiality and to safeguard all information associated with the tester-test taker relationship.
- Confidentiality cannot be absolute, especially where the records concern students who may be competing for admissions and appointments. A careful balance must be maintained between preserving confidentiality as a fundamental aspect of the language tester's professional duty and the wider responsibility the tester has to society.
- Similarly, in appropriate cases, the language tester's professional colleagues also have a right to access data of test takers other than their own ion order to improve the service the profession offers. In such cases, those given access to data should agree to maintain confidentiality.
- Test taker data collected from sources other than the test taker directly (for example from teachers of students under test) are subject to the same principles of confidentiality.
- There may be statutory requirements on disclosure, for example where the language tester is called as an expert witness in a law court or tribunal. In such circumstances, the language tester is released from his/her professional duty to confidentiality.

Principle 3

Language testers should adhere to all relevant ethical principles embodied in national and international guidelines when undertaking any trial, experiment, treatment or other research activity.

Annotation

- Language testing progress depends on research, which necessarily involves the participation of human subjects. This research shall conform to generally accepted principles of academic inquiry, be based on a thorough knowledge of the professional literature; and be planned and executed according to the highest standards.
- All research must be justified; that is proposed studies shall be reasonably expected to provide answers to questions posed.

- The human rights of the research subject shall always take precedence over the interests of science or society.
- Where there are likely discomforts or risks to the research subject, the benefits of that research should be taken into account but must not be used in themselves to justify such discomforts or risks. If unforeseeable harmful effects occur, the research should always be stopped or modified.
- An independent Ethics Committee should evaluate all research proposals in order to ensure that studies conform to the highest scientific and ethical standards.
- Relevant information about the aims, methods, risks and discomforts of the research shall be given to the subject in advance. The information shall be conveyed in such a way that it is fully understood. Consent shall be free, without pressure, coercion or duress.
- The subject shall be free to refuse to participate in or to withdraw from, the research at any time prior to publication of research results. Such refusal shall not jeopardise the subject's treatment.
- Special care shall be taken with regard to obtaining prior consent in the case of subjects who are in dependent relationships (for example, students, the elderly, proficiency challenged learners).
- In the case of a minor, consent shall be obtained from a parent or guardian but also from the child if he is of sufficient maturity and understanding.
- Confidential information obtained in research shall not be used for purposes other than THOSE specified in the approved research protocol.
- Publication of research results shall be truthful and accurate.
- Publication of research reports shall not permit identification of the subjects who have been involved.

Principle 4

Language testers shall not allow the misuse of their professional knowledge or skills, in so far as they are able.

Annotation

- Language testers shall not knowingly use their professional knowledge or skills to advance purposes inimical to their test takers' interests. When the progress of the tester's intervention is not directly to the benefit of the test takers (for example, when they are asked to act as trial subjects for a proficiency test designed for some other situation), its nature shall be made absolutely clear.
- Non-conformity with a society's prevailing moral, religious etc. values, or status as an unwelcome migrant, shall not be the determining factor in assessing language ability.

- Whatever the legal circumstances, language testers shall not participate, either directly or indirectly in the practice of torture or other forms of cruel, inhuman or degrading punishment (see Declaration of Tokyo 1975).

Principle 5

Language testers shall continue to develop their professional knowledge, sharing this knowledge with colleagues and other language professionals.

Annotation

- Continued learning and advancing one's knowledge are fundamental to the professional role; failure to do so constitutes a disservice to test takers.
- Language testers shall make use of the various methods of continuing education that are available to them. These may involve participation in continuing language testing programmes and professional conferences, and the regular reading of relevant professional publications.
- Language testers shall take the opportunity to interact with colleagues and other relevant language professionals as an important means of developing their professional knowledge.
- Language testers shall share new knowledge with colleagues by publication in recognized professional journals or at meetings.
- Language testers shall be expected to contribute to the education and professional development of language testers in training and to the drawing up of guidelines for the core requirements of that training.
- Language testers shall be prepared to contribute to the education of students in the WIDER language professions.

Principle 6

Language testers shall share the responsibility of upholding the integrity of the language testing profession.

Annotation

- Language testers shall promote and enhance the integrity of their profession by fostering a sense of trust and mutual responsibility among colleagues. In the event of differences of opinion, viewpoints should be expressed with candour and respect rather than by mutual denigration.
- Language testers develop and exercise norms on behalf of society. As such theirs is a privileged position which brings with it an obligation to maintain appropriate personal and moral standards in their professional

practice, and in those aspects of their personal life which may reflect upon the integrity of that practice.

- Language testers who become aware of unprofessional conduct by a colleague shall take appropriate action; this may include a report to the relevant authorities.
- Failure to uphold this Code of Ethics will be regarded with the utmost seriousness and could lead to severe penalties including withdrawal of ILTA membership.

Principle 7

Language testers in their societal roles shall strive to improve the quality of language testing, assessment and teaching services, promote the just allocation of those services and contribute to the education of society regarding language learning and language proficiency.

Annotation

- Language testers have a particular duty to promote the improvement of language testing provision/services in that many of their test takers are disenfranchised and lack power on account of their non-native speaker status.
- Language testers shall be prepared by virtue of their knowledge and experience to advise those responsible for the provision of language testing services.
- Language testers shall be prepared to act as advocates and join with others in ensuring that language testing test takers have available to them the best possible language testing service.
- Language testers shall be prepared to work with advisory, statutory, voluntary and commercial bodies that have a role in the provision of language testing services.
- Language testers shall take appropriate action if services, by reason of fiscal restriction or otherwise, fall below minimal standards.

    Exceptionally, language testers may have to dissociate themselves from such services provided that this is not harmful to their test takers.
- Language testers shall be prepared to interpret and disseminate relevant scientific information and established professional opinions to society. In so doing, language testers shall clarify their status as either spokespersons for a recognised professional body or not. If the views expressed are contrary to those generally held, they shall so indicate.
- It is reasonable for language testers to make scientifically substantiated contributions to public debate on sensitive socio-political issues, such as race, disadvantage and child rearing.
- Language testers shall differentiate between their role as educators based on professional knowledge and their role as citizens.

- In fulfilling their responsibilities under this principle, language testers shall take care to avoid self-promotion and the denigration of colleagues.
- Language testers shall make clear that they do not claim (and are not seen to claim) that they alone possess all the relevant knowledge.

Principle 8

Language testers shall be mindful of their obligations to the society within which they work, while recognising that those obligations may on occasion conflict with their responsibilities to their test takers and to other stakeholders.

Annotation   .

- When test results are obtained on behalf of institutions (government departments, professional bodies, universities, schools, companies) language testers have an obligation to report those results accurately, however unwelcome they may be to the test takers and other stakeholders (families, prospective employers etc.).
- As members of the society in which they work, language testers should recognise their obligation to the testing requirements of that society, even when they may not themselves agree with them. Where their disagreement is of sufficient strength to qualify as a conscientious objection, they should have the right to withdraw their professional services.

Principle 9

Language testers shall regularly consider the potential effects, both short and long term on all stakeholders of their projects, reserving the right to withhold their professional services on the grounds of conscience.

Annotation

- As professionals, language testers have the responsibility to evaluate the ethical consequences of the projects submitted to them. While they cannot consider all possible eventualities, they should engage in a thorough evaluation of the likely consequences and, where those consequences are in their view professionally unacceptable, withdraw their services. In such cases, they should as a matter of course consult with fellow language testers to determine how far their view is shared, always reserving the right, where their colleagues take a different view, to make an individual stand on the grounds of conscience.

Appendix B

Code of practice*

Principles for assessment and reporting

(Formulated by the Australian Council of State School Organizations and the Australian Parents' Council)

1. Parents are entitled to continuing, quality information regarding their children's education through a variety of mechanisms.
2. Any form of assessment should be integral to the curriculum and designed to inform, support, and improve learning outcomes.
3. Assessment and reporting processes should make provision for parent and student input about teaching and learning.
4. Parents and their organizations must have an active role in developing and implementing assessment and reporting policies and processes at the school, the system, the state and the nation levels.
5. Schools, systems and governments, state and federal, must make explicit and public the purposes for which they wish to collect assessment data.
6. Assessment data must not be used for the purpose of establishing and publishing competitive judgements about schools, systems, states or territories.
7. Parents must be informed by all these who seek such data about student performance of the uses to which such information will be put.
8. Data collected from students in schools should be used in accordance with its stated purposes. Any other subsequent uses should be specifically negotiated.
9. Individual student assessments are confidential to the student, his or her parents and appropriate school staff.
10. Parents have the right to withdraw their children from specific system, statewide and national testing.

* Quoted in Lynch (1997)

11.   Assessment data for statewide or national purposes should be collected by statistically valid, light sampling procedures only.
12.   Appropriate appeal mechanisms should be established and made public to protect the rights of students and parents in matters of student assessment and reporting at the school, state and national level.

Principles for evaluating language development

1.   What and how we evaluate must be consistent with what we value about language and language development.
2.   Evaluation strategies must evaluate what they set out to evaluate (e.g. to check spelling by having the student select the correct spelling of a word from a list of alternative spellings tells nothing about how that student would spell that same word in a writing situation).
3.   The purpose of evaluation is to inform the learners, teachers and parents. It thus must be descriptive.
4.   Learning is ongoing, therefore evaluation must be ongoing.
5.   Language is learned in use; language use is context related. Language evaluation therefore must occur in authentic contexts.
6.   As language use relates to language experience, an externally administered evaluation procedure may evaluate the teaching programme more than it evaluates the student's language competence.
7.   Language learning is developmental. It involves experimentation and approximation. Language assessment must reveal the student's developing understandings.
8.   Learning to control the surface features of a language does not necessarily occur at the same rate as learning to control the functions of a language.
9.   Student self-evaluation is an important part of the evaluation process.

(Wilson, 1995: 3)

Codes of this sort could protect the test takers and at the same time limit the powers of those who produce, introduce or misuse tests.

Bibliography

ACTFL (1986) *ACTFL Proficiency Guidelines*. Hastings-on-Hudson, NY: American Council on the Teaching of Foreign Languages.

Alderson, J.C., Clapham, C. and Wall, D. (1995) *Language Test Construction and Evaluation*. Cambridge: Cambridge University Press.

Alderson, J.C. and Hamp-Lyons, L. (1996) TOEFL preparation courses: A study of washback. *Language Testing*, **13** (3): 280–97.

Alderson, J.C. and Wall, D. (1993) Does washback exist? *Applied Linguistics*, **14** (2): 115–29.

Banks, J. (1998) The lives and values of researchers: Implications for educating citizens in a multicultural society. *Educational Researchers*, **27** (7): 4–17.

Ben-Rafael, E. (1994) *Language, Identity, and Social Division: The Case of Israel*. Oxford: Clarendon Press.

Ben-Rafael, E. and Brosh, H. (1991) A sociological study of second language diffusion: The obstacles to Arabic teaching in the Israeli school. *Language Problem and Language Planning*, **15**: 1–23.

Bernstein, B. (1982) Codes, modalities and the process of cultural reproduction: A model. In M. Apple (ed.) *Cultural and Economic Reproduction in Education*. London: Routledge & Kegan Paul.

Bernstein, B. (1986) On pedagogical discourse. In J. Richardson (ed.) *Handbook for Theory and Research for the Sociology of Education*. New York: Greenwood Press.

Bourdieu, P. (1991) *Language and Symbolic Power*. Cambridge, MA: Harvard University Press.

Broadfoot, P. (1996) *Education, Assessment and Society: A Sociological Analysis*. Buckingham: Open University Press.

Byrnes, H. (1987) Second language acquisition: Insights from a proficiency orientation. In Heidi Byrnes and Michale Canale (eds) *Defining and Developing Proficiency Guidelines. Implementations and Concepts*. ACTFL Foreign Language Education Series, vol. 17. Lincolnwood, IL: National Textbook Company, pp. 107–32.

Cheng, L. (1998) Impact of a public English examination change on students' perceptions and attitudes toward their English learning. *Studies in Educational Evaluation*, **24** (3): 279–301.

Clinton, W. (1997) State of the Union Address, 4 February.

Darling-Hammond, L. (1994) Performance-based assessment and educational equity. *Harvard Educational Review*, **64** (1): 5–30.

Davies, A. (1997) Demands of being professional in language testing. *Language Testing*, **14** (3): 328–39.

Elder, C. (1997) What does test bias have to do with fairness? *Language Testing*, **14** (3): 261–77.

Ellul, J. (1964) *The Technological Society*. New York: Vintage Books.

Eribon, D. (1991) *Michel Foucault* (translated by Betsy Wing). Cambridge, Mass.: Cambridge University Press.

Ferman, I. (1998) *The impact of a new English foreign language oral matriculation test on the educational system*. MA Thesis, School of Education, Tel Aviv University.

Fetterman, D., Kaftarian, S. and Wandersman, A. (1996) *Empowerment Evaluation*. Sage Publication.

Fillmore, C. (1981) Ideal reader and real reader. In D. Tanners (ed.) *Analysing Discourse: Text and Talk*. Washington, DC: Georgetown University Press, pp. 248–70. (Georgetown University Round Table on Languages and Linguistics, 1981.)

Foucault, M. (1979) *Discipline and Punish*. New York: Vintage Books.

Foucault, M. (1991) *Remarks on Marx. Conversations with Duccio Trombadori* (translated by R. James Goldstein and James Cascaito). Brooklyn NY: Semiotext (E).

Fredriksen, J. and Collins, A. (1989) A system approach to educational testing. *Educational Researcher*, **18**: 27–32.

Freedman, W.S. (1993) Linking large-scale testing and classroom portfolio assessments of student writing. *Educational Assessment*, **1** (1): 27–52.

Freedman, W.S. (1995) Exam-based reform stifles student writing in the U.K. *Educational Leadership*, **52** (6): 26–9.

Freire, P. (1985) *The Politics of Education*. South Hadley, MA: Bergin & Gravey.

Gefen, R. (1983) Reliability in the English Bagrut Test. *English Teacher's Journal* (Israel), **29**: 14–20.

Gipps, C.V. (1994) *Beyond Testing: Towards a Theory of Educational Assessment*. London: Falmer Press.

Giroux, H. (1995) Language, difference, and curriculum theory: Beyond the politics and clarity. In P. McLaren and J. Giarelli (eds) *Critical Theory and Educational Research*. New York: State University of New York Press.

Hamp-Lyons, L. (1997) Washback, impact and validity: Ethical concerns. *Language Testing*, **14** (3): 295–303.

Hanson, F.A. (1993) *Testing Testing: Social Consequences of the Examined Life*. Berkeley, CA: University of California Press.

Hawthorne, L. (1996) The politicisation of English: The case of the *step* test and the Chinese students. In F. Wigglesworth and C. Elder (eds) *Australian Review of Applied Linguistics, Series S*, **13**: 13–32.

Hawthorne, L. (1997) The political dimension of English language testing in Australia. *Language Testing*, **14** (3): 248–60.

Horovitz, N. (1986) *Policy and planning in the teaching of English in Israel*. MA thesis, English, Bar Ilan University, Ramat Gan.

House, E.R. (1990) Ethics of evaluation studies. In H.J. Walberg and G.D. Haertel (eds) *The International Encyclopedia of Educational Evaluation*. Oxford: Pergamon Press, pp. 91–4.

House, E. (1998) *Schools for Sale*. New York, NY: Teacher College Press.

Howe, K.R. (1994) Standards, assessment, and equality of educational opportunity. *Educational Researcher*, **23**: 27–33.

ILTA (2000) *Code of Ethics for Foreign/Second Language Testing*. Hong Kong International Language Testing Association.

Joint Committee on Standards for Educational Evaluation (1981) *Standards for Evaluation of Educational Programs, Projects and Materials*. New York: McGraw-Hill.

Koretz, D., Madaus, G., Haertal, E. and Veaton, B.A. (1992) *National Educational Standards and Testing: A Response to the Recommendations of the National Council in Education Standards and Testing*. Santa Monica, CA: Rand Corporation.

Kraemer, R. (1993) Social psychological factors related to the study of Arabic among Israeli Jewish high school students: A test of Gardner's socioeducational model. *Studies in Second Language Acquisition*, **15** (1): 83–106.

Kramsch, C. (1993) *Context and Culture in Language Teaching*. Oxford: Oxford University Press.

Latham, H. (1877) *On the Action of Examinations Considered as a Means of Selection*. Cambridge: Deighton, Bell & Co.

Lemke, J. (1995) *Textual Politics: Discourse and Social Dynamics*. London: Taylor & Francis.

Lo, M. (1997) *A critical analysis of a Hong Kong English exam*. MA Thesis presented to the School for International Training, Vermont.

Lynch, B. (1997) In search of the ethical test. *Language Testing*, **14** (3): 315–27.

MacIntyre, A.C. (1984) *After Virtue* (2nd edn). Notre Dame, IN: University of Notre Dame Press.

Madaus, G. (1990) *Testing as a Social Technology. The Inaugural Annual Boise Lecture on Education and Public Policy*. Boston, MA: Boston College.

Madaus, G. (1994) A technological and historical consideration of equity issues associated with proposals to change the nations testing policy. *Harvard Educational Review*, **64** (1): 76–95.

Madaus, G. (in press) *Educational Testing as Technology. National Board on Educational Testing and Public Policy*. Lynch School of Education, Boston College Statements. Volume 5.

Marisi, P. (1994) Questions of regionalism in native speakers OPI performance: The French Canadian Experience. *Foreign Language Annals*, **27** (4): 505–21.

McGahern, J. (1977) *The Dark*. New York: Quartet.

McLuhan, M. (1962) *The Gutenberg Galaxy: The Making of Typographic Man*. Toronto: University of Toronto Press.

McNamara, T. (1990) Item response theory and the validation of an ESP test for health professionals. *Language Testing*, **7** (1): 31–51.

McNamara, T. (1997) Policy and social considerations in language assessment. In B. Grabe (ed.) *Annual Review of Applied Linguistics*, **18**: 304–19.

McNeil, L. (1986) *Contradictions of Control*. New York: Routledge.

Messick, S. (1981) Evidence and Ethics in the Evaluation of Tests. *Educational Researcher*, **10**: 9–20.

Messick, S. (1989) Validity. In R.L. Linn (ed.) *Educational measurement* (3rd edn). Washington, DC: The American Council on Education and the National Council on Measurement in Education, pp. 13–103.

Messick, S. (1994) The interplay of evidence and consequences in the validation of performance assessments. *Educational Researcher*, **23**: 13–23.

Messick, S. (1996) Validity and washback in language testing. *Language Testing*, **13** (4): 241–57.

Moss, P. (1996) Enlarging the dialogue in educational measurement: Voices from interpretive research traditions. *Educational Researcher*, **25** (1): 20–8.

Nevo, D. (1996) *School Based Evaluation*. Oxford: Pergamon Press.

Nevo, D. and Shohamy, E. (1986) Evaluation standards for the assessment of alternative testing methods: an application. *Studies in Educational Evaluation*, **12** (2): 149–58.

New York Times, The (1998) Massachusetts retreats on threshold for teacher test, flunking nearly 60 per cent. (1 July).

Nitko, A. (1989) Designing tests that are integrated with instruction. In R.L. Linn (ed.) *Educational Measurement* (3rd edition). Englewood Cliffs, NJ: Prentice-Hall, pp. 447–74.

Nitko, A. (1996) *Educational Assessment of Students*. Englewood Cliffs, NJ: Prentice-Hall.

Noah, E. and Eckstein, M. (1992) *Examinations in Comparative and International Studies*. Oxford: Pergamon Press.

Noam, G. (1996) Assessment at a Crossroads: Conversation. *Harvard Educational Review*, **66**: 631–57.

Ormsby, H. (1998) The language tester and indigenous languages. Paper presented at the conference on The Social Responsibility of the Language Tester, University of Ottawa, 5 July 1998.

Oxenham, J. (1984) *Education versus Qualifications?* London: Allen and Unwin.

Peirce, B.N. and Stein, P. (1995) Why the 'monkeys passage' bombed: tests, genres, and teaching. *Harvard Educational Review*, **54** (1): 50–65.

Pennycook, A. (1994) *The Cultural Politics of English as an International Language*. London and New York: Longman.

Phillipson, R. (1992) *Linguistic Imperialism*. Oxford: Oxford University Press.

Punch, M. (1994) Politics and ethics in qualitative research. In N.K. Denzin and Y.S. Lincoln (eds) *Handbook of qualitative research*. Thousand Oaks, CA: Sage, pp. 83–97.

Schwandt, T. (1989) Recapturing moral discourse in evaluation. *Educational Researcher*, **18** (8): 11–16.

Schwartz, T. (1999) The test under stress. *The New York Times Magazine*, 10 January, p. 30.

Shepard, L. (1991) Psychometricians' beliefs about learning. *Educational Researcher*, **20** (7): 2–9.

Shohamy, E. (1985) *A Practical Handbook in Language Testing for the Second Language Teacher*. Shaked, Ramat Aviv, Israel.

Shohamy, E. (1991) International perspectives of foreign language testing systems and policy. *ACTFL Annual Review of Foreign Languages*, Vol. 16. The American Council on the Teaching of Foreign Languages, National Textbook Co., IL, pp. 91–107.

Shohamy, E. (1993) *The power of tests: The impact of language tests on teaching and learning*. Washington, DC: The National Foreign Language Center at Johns Hopkins University.

Shohamy, E. (1994) The use of language tests for power and control. In J. Alatis (ed.) *Georgetown University Round Table on Language and Linguistics*. Washington, DC: Georgetown University Press, pp. 57–72.

Shohamy, E. (1995) Language testing: Matching assessment procedures with language knowledge. In M. Birenbaum and F. Dochy (eds) *Alternatives in assessment of achievements, learning processes and prior knowledge*. Boston, MA: Kluwer Academic Publishing, pp. 142–60.

Shohamy, E. (1997) Testing methods, testing consequences: are they ethical? Are they fair? *Language Testing*, **14** (3): 340–9.

Shohamy, E. (1998) Critical language testing and beyond. *Studies in Educational Evaluation*, **24** (4): 331–45.

Shohamy, E. and Donitsa-Schmidt, S. (1998) *Jews vs. Arabs: Language attitudes and stereotypes*. Report submitted to the Shtainmintz Center for Peace, Tel Aviv University.

Shohamy, E., Donitsa-Schmidt, S. and Ferman, I. (1996) Test impact revisited: Washback effect over time. *Language Testing*, **13** (3): 298–317.

Shohamy, E., Reves, T. and Bejarano, Y. (1986) Introducing a new comprehensive test of oral proficiency. *English Language Teaching Journal*, **40** (3): 212–20.

Smith, M.L. (1991) Put to test: The effects of external testing on teachers. *Educational Researcher*, **20**: 8–11.

Spolsky, B. (1995) *Measured Words: The Development of Objective Language Testing*. Oxford: Oxford University Press.

Spolsky, B. (1997) The ethics of gatekeeping tests: What have we learned in a hundred years? *Language Testing*, **14** (3): 242–7.

Spolsky, B. (1998) What is the user's perspective in language testing? Paper presented at the Colloquium, *The State of the Art in Language Testing: The Users' Perspective*, National Foreign Language Center, The Johns Hopkins University, Washington DC, 15 June.

Steinberg, J. (1999) Stress test. *New York Times, Education Life*, 3 January, p. 18.

Steiner, J. (1995) *Changes in the English Bagrut Exam*. Jesusalem: State of Israel Ministry of Education, Culture and Sport, English Inspectorate.

Tollefson, J. (1995) Introduction: Language policy, power, and inequality. In J. Tollefson (ed.) *Power and Inequality in Language Education*. London: Cambridge University Press.

US Department of Education (1992) *World Class Standards for American Education*, Washington, D.C.

Valdes, G. and Figueroa, R. (1996) *Bilingualism and Testing: A Special Case of Bias*. Norwood, NJ: Ablex Publishing Corp.

Wall, D. (1996) Introducing new tests into traditional systems: Insights from general education and from innovation theory. *Language Testing*, **13**: 334–54.

Wall, D. and Alderson, J.C. (1993) Examining washback: The Sri Lankan impact study. *Language Testing*, **10** (1): 41–69.

Watanabe, Y. (1996) Does grammar translation come from the entrance examination? Preliminary findings from classroom-based research. *Language Testing*, **13**: 318–33.

Weiss, C.H. (1977) *Using Social Research in Public Policy Making*. MA: Lexington Books.

Wilson, L. (1995) Principles for evaluating language development. *NLLIA Network Notes*, **8** (3).

Winner, L. (1986) *The Whale and the reactor: A search for limits in an age of high technology*. Chicago: The University of Chicago Press.

Zack, I. (1982) *Alternative Assessment for Matriculation Examination: A Feasible Model*. Internal document (in Hebrew) School of Education, Tel Aviv University.

Index